CREATIVE WRITING

The Essential Guide

Tim Atkinson

Creative Writing – The Essential Guide is also available in accessible formats for people with any degree of visual impairment. The large print edition and eBook (with accessibility features enabled) are available from Need2Know. Please let us know if there are any special features you require and we will do our best to accommodate your needs.

First published in Great Britain in 2011 by
Need2Know
Remus House
Coltsfoot Drive
Peterborough
PE2 9BF
Telephone 01733 898103
Fax 01733 313524
www.need2knowbooks.co.uk

Contents

Introduction

It might be a cliché to say that 'everyone has a book in them' but if the number of people attending writing classes, taking writing courses and responding to the familiar 'Why not be a writer?' ads in newspapers is anything to go by then there must be more than a hint of truth about it. Every year more and more people take up writing either as a rewarding hobby, a means of self-discovery, a vehicle for self-expression or as a possible means of earning a living.

But if the chances of hitting the *Sunday Times* best-seller list are slim, then chances of making a decent living out of writing are even slimmer. It's estimated that 90% of writers earn just 10% of the income generated by all writing, and breaking into that top 10% who earn the lion's share of royalties and fees is not going to be easy.

Of course if you're a genius with a rare writing talent and either the luck or the connections to get yourself noticed, you'll not need this or any other guide book. If you're a celebrity with a kiss-and-tell story, you won't even need to write the book yourself if you don't want to. But if, on the other hand, you're one of the many thousands of would-be authors serious about developing your talent as a creative writer and if you'd like ideas and tips for getting your work finished, accepted and published, then *Creative Writing – The Essential Guide* is the book for you.

Whether you're an established writer or a beginner, whether you see your work as a potential source of income, the road to stardom or as a personally rewarding spare-time occupation, you'll find plenty in this book to help you through the process of writing from the ideas stage through to the finish-line and on (should you wish) to the threshold of publication.

By the end of this book you will be able to use a variety of different prompts for your ideas even when you're not feeling inspired. You'll have a better idea of your strengths and weaknesses as a writer; you'll be able to look at your own work dispassionately and you'll have the skills to edit and improve your work – making it the very best that it can be. You'll also gain important knowledge about the different genres and disciplines of creative writing and – crucially –

you'll have an idea of which outlet is the best for your own writing talent. Finally, if your goal is publication, you'll learn about the process of preparing your work ready for submission, including essential tips about style, layout and the etiquette of submitting a manuscript to both an agent and a publisher.

Chapter One

Getting the Habit

In this chapter we'll look at capturing, recording and developing your writing ideas. We'll discuss methods of adapting the unnatural business of writing to our normal ways of thinking in order to get the most out of moments of inspiration.

Writing is something we all do, everyday. Whether it's shopping lists, blog posts, poetry or accumulating chapters of the next great novel, we're all at it. And it's amazing how many people *want* to do it – more often, for longer, for money, for pleasure. Whatever your motivation – and whatever style or genre you're most interested in – I hope this book helps you take a few more steps towards achieving your goal.

'Never shut the door on a muse: she just won't be there when you need to open it again.'

W.N.Herbert, Professor of Poetry and Creative Writing, Newcastle University.

Exercise 1.1

Before reading any further, it would be worth considering for a moment what your personal writing goals are. What do you hope to achieve, and what do you hope to have gained by the end of this book?

A brief history of shopping lists

Writing is actually quite an unnatural activity. Going back to shopping lists for a moment, the earliest examples of the 'written' word are actually just that – or more precisely, the inventories made by ancient Babylonian merchants. The cuneiform tablets on which they kept tally of their stock are thought to be the first examples anywhere of the written word, so the next time you're writing a shopping list remember that you're writing a little bit of history!

Human beings, though, have been around a good deal longer than the seven thousand or so years since the birth of writing. In evolutionary terms our brains haven't yet adapted to the written word, certainly not as it's normally written – in neat lines on pieces of crisp, white paper. Yet so much of what we do depends on words, and an ability to manipulate them successfully is counted pretty universally as an important indication of intelligence.

But our ideas don't tend to organise themselves in tidy sentences, nor into a logical sequence; still less do they lend themselves to being written down. This is why, sometimes, ideas that seem so brilliant in your head can look so disappointing when you see them on the page. And this, more than anything else, is the hard work of creative writing. If your bright idea is the 1% inspiration, transferring it successfully to paper is definitely 99% perspiration. Thanks for that equation, Mr Edison!

'Writing is actually quite an unnatural activity.'

That, then, is going to be the main business of this creative writing guide: making the best of your ideas and improving your ability to communicate successfully with the reader. But I suppose we should at least start by considering where ideas come from in the first place. Staring at an empty sheet of paper or a blank computer screen is seldom very productive, so to begin with let's try something different.

Think of an event in your life that you can recall vividly. It needn't be a dramatic, life-changing or epoch-making situation, merely something that you can recall quite easily and in a reasonable amount of detail. What I want you to do, as you remember this event, is *hear* the sounds you heard, *see* the things you saw, *feel* the things you felt, *smell* the things you smelt and *touch* the things you touched at the time of this experience.

Exercise 1.2

Now, for your second writing exercise I want you to write a 'shopping list' of single words or phrases – nothing like a complete sentence – that come to mind as you consider the event you've just recalled. Make no conscious attempt to 'think' about it or to edit what you write; just record whatever comes to mind and keep the process going for as long as it feels comfortable.

If you were asked to remember the last really good film that you'd seen, the chances of you immediately recalling the beginning of the narrative and then re-playing all the key events in sequence would be pretty small. I suppose there are some people who do that. But for most of us, what we tend to recall are the key incidents, flash-backs, dramatic sequences and strong visual images.

It's the same with memorable occasions in our lives. We don't remember the past as a linear sequence of events with mundane and routine details interspersed with the occasional act of high drama: what we remember is the drama.

Now, what has all this got to do with writing? Well, everything – especially at the 'ideas' stage of writing. What you need to develop is a means of recording your ideas without getting bogged down with all the details. If you want to write a novel, don't start with a piece of paper headed 'Chapter One'. That very rarely works. Instead, keep a notebook, write down odd snatches of dialogue that you imagine or that you overhear, make 'shopping list' type notes of incidents you want to write about and most importantly – don't think too closely at this stage about where it's going or what it might become. Just make writing – sketching, really – something of a habit.

What would a writer say?

Ok, so you're jotting down all sorts of things in that nice notebook that you keep especially for the purpose, or else you're scribbling on the backs of envelopes or any other scrap of paper. You're not editing or 'grammatising' anything. You're simply getting the ideas down, shopping-list style. Your life as a writer has begun. The ideas will build, the notebook will begin to bulge or that pile of paper will grow steadily taller. And the time will come when you know that you're ready to start developing the material you've been gathering.

Great artists do this all the time; they carry sketch books with them and quickly draw a scene or detail that inspires them. Leonardo da Vinci was probably the world's greatest note-book scribbler, and his apparently random jottings, drawings and equations are a record of a mind brimming with ideas. It seemed to come so easily to him. It may not come so easily to the rest of us. So what happens when the notebook pages start to be neglected?

'We don't remember the past as a linear sequence of events with mundane and routine details interspersed with the occasional act of high drama: what we remember is the drama.'

Well, 'write what you know' is the oft-quoted advice. And to the extent that if you're going to write about anything you have to know about it, I suppose that must be true. But you don't – of course – have to know about it *before* you start to think about your writing. Research – the stuff of non-fiction writing of all kinds – is an essential part of the writing process and by 'research' I don't mean sitting in a library for hours or endlessly surfing the Internet.

I remember the playwright Jack Rosenthal talking once about why he'd turned down a paid position that would have meant him working office hours. 'I'd miss standing at the school gates waiting for my children to come out of school,' he explained. 'And that's where I hear some of my best lines.'

The point is this: we're all living lives that we can use as a source of inspiration or research if we try. Those trees you were looking at earlier, laced with fresh May blossom. What would *a writer* say about them? Now that's a notoriously difficult question and even the playwright Dennis Potter, in his final illness, resorted to describing the apple tree outside his window in Ross-on-Wye as having the 'blossomiest' blossom he had ever seen. But *you're* a writer: so what words would *you* use to describe it? And remember, you're not writing in sentences. Not yet.

> 'My father writes, my grandfather was a writer and editor of the Catholic Herald, his father and grandfather had been writers. So writing was in the family.'
>
> Guy de la Bédoyère, author and historian

Exercise 1.3

Have a go at this now. It needn't be blossom, or trees or anything from nature. Just pick an object and describe it – shopping list style – using whatever words occur to you. Keep the object vividly in front of you, either in your imagination, on a photo or looking out of the window. And don't worry if the words seem odd or strange or if you think that no-one else would understand why that particular word is on your list. Just write!

Of course the time will come when you've got to make those ideas intelligible to other people. And although some of the most satisfying books leave a little bit to the imagination, we don't want to make the reader work too hard. This is where the real craft of writing begins.

Exercise 1.4

Go back to the list you made in response to exercise 1.2. Read the words again a couple of times. Now try, in your head, to re-create the narrative (story) of the experience you were recalling. Use your list to write a paragraph describing in detail what happened. Don't comment on it or explain anything at this stage (and *don't edit!*). Simply let your mind take you in whichever direction it desires. Don't worry if you appear to be moving further away from the original experience. Let your imagination take you where it wants to.

Now, depending on your mood/the time of day/your children/the postman, that exercise can either last for hours or else fizzle out after a few seconds like a cheap firework. But don't be disheartened. In fact, be pleased. Either extreme isn't just possible, it's normal – and so is everything in-between. Make the most of the days when the ideas flow and things come easily, but be prepared for the days when they don't. And don't give up – go back. If you can, try doing the last three exercises in this chapter several times; it should yield interesting – and different – results on each occasion.

Well, that's the end of chapter one. I hope you've enjoyed reading; that you've learnt something and – more than anything – that you keep reading and, of course, keep writing!

Summing Up

- *Don't write!*
  Writers write, right? Wrong! Humans haven't been writing very long; our brains aren't adapted to the ways of words on paper (or computer). To be a successful writer and to capture and preserve your best ideas, you've got to adapt to the way your brain works: make lists, doodle, brainstorm. Don't, whatever you do, write ideas down in full sentences.

- *Get the habit.*
  Don't just stand and gaze at that beautiful sunset, or rage at that ignorant boy-racer at the traffic lights. Ask yourself: what words would a writer use to write about this experience? Those words may not come easily at first, but it's a habit – once acquired – that will be difficult to break.

- *Don't edit.*
  Not yet, anyway. Editing is as important as (if not more so than) the act of writing, but as the Bible says, there is a time and a place. And this isn't it.

Chapter Two

Identify Yourself

In this chapter we'll look at how a writer can develop a unique 'voice' and examine the view that what you write about is as important in defining your identity as an author as your style of writing.

We're all different. In spite of what I had one of my characters say in my novel 'Writing Therapy', not even identical twins with their exactly-matching DNA turn out to have precisely the same personality. Experiences, however subtly, differ; perspectives change; interpretations vary. It's well-known that witnesses to an accident can and often do give completely different accounts of what they've seen. And yet they've 'seen' the same thing.

On the face of it then, developing your own voice as an author should be easy. There's no-one quite like you, who thinks the way you do and sees the world through your eyes, interpreting it from your experience. So what you write and the way you write it should be equally unique. But it often isn't, especially at the start of a writing career. And the reasons aren't hard to find.

On the shelf

If there's one thing wannabe writers are told time and time again, it's 'read, read, read'. And that's good advice: you can't help but learn from reading well-written words in a carefully crafted setting and no-one can ever do too much reading. But *what* you read and *why* you read it is the crucial thing to consider when you're writing. How you read is a subject I'll be talking more about in the next chapter, so for now let's consider the two 'W's.

'We're all different. In spite of what I had one of my characters say in my novel 'Writing Therapy', not even identical twins with their exactly-matching DNA turn out to have precisely the same personality.'

Exercise 2.1

What you read . . .

Take a few moments to consider the kind of things that you like reading. Is there a particular genre or style of writing you enjoy? How catholic are your tastes? And how do you choose the books you read?

Looking at people's bookshelves is a great pastime, and you can tell a lot about a person by the kind of books they read. On my bedside table at the moment, for example, there's a book called *The English Chorister: A Survey*; Lynn Truss's *Eats, Shoots and Leaves*; *Truant*, by Horatio Clare and *Paperweight*, by Stephen Fry. No fiction at the moment, although *The Kite Runner* is top of the 'to read' pile.

What does that reveal? Well, an interest in the English choral tradition for a start, as well as a tendency to 'catch up' long after the fuss about a book (Kite Runner; Lynn Truss) has died down. It also reveals the kind of books I read because I think I might learn something from them (Horatio Clare) and this little exercise has a dual purpose.

Over the next few days I'd like you to consider which single book you'd recommend as being of interest and use to a budding writer. I don't mean 'How To' books like this one as much as those that you think are examples of really good practice. Once you've made your choice, think about aspects of the writer's style and subject matter that are like your own.

Exercise 2.2

Now I'd like you to consider the second 'W': why do you read what you do? For this task I want you to consider not only specific books or subjects or a style of writing you admire, but also the question of what purpose reading serves in your own life.

Is it relaxation? Escapism? Education? Or all three?

If you think we've strayed from the subject of this chapter, think again. Author-voice is probably a function of what we read as much as who we are, and it's inevitable that we'll try to emulate our favourite authors, either in style, subject matter or both. That isn't necessarily a bad thing. Imitation is the sincerest form of flattery, so they say. But what *is* most certainly a bad thing in any form of writing is relying on cliché (as I've just done!) and that's what we'll examine now.

Hot off the press

Interestingly, the word 'cliché' and its sister 'stereotype' have their origin in the publishing and writing industry. In the old days of hot metal printing presses and moveable type, frequently-used phrases were preserved from one job to the next in order to save them being set up one letter at a time from scratch. (Oops! *From scratch* . . . . Of course I mean 'from the beginning' rather than the original sporting definition of *from scratch*, which is 'to start with no advantage'.)

There's nothing inherently wrong with clichés – the reason they persist is that they sometimes provide useful shorthand phrases for common experiences, just as they once provided useful short-cuts for hot metal printers. But they're often over-used to the point where their meaning changes and becomes unclear, and if there's one thing you don't want as a writer, it's misunderstanding. In addition, don't we owe it to our readers to be different? If all we're capable of doing is *churning out* (oops, there I go again!) material that's identical to other people's, what's the point of writing anything at all?

'The word 'cliché' and its sister 'stereotype' have their origin in the publishing and writing industry.'

Exercise 2.3

For each of the following clichéd phrases and expressions, try and write your own unique alternative. Try to be imaginative; think beyond the obvious and be original.

a. A picture paints a thousand words.

b. As happy as a pig in muck.

c. To start from scratch.

d. Out of the frying pan into the fire.

e. Don't throw the baby out with the bathwater

f. Never look a gift-horse in the mouth.

g. Up and down like a yo-yo.

'You don't have to re-invent language or re-define the form like a latter-day James Joyce to be different from the rest. Just be yourself. Only you see the world your way.'

You don't have to re-invent language or re-define the form like a latter-day James Joyce to be different from the rest. Just be yourself. Only *you* see the world your way; make a real effort to find the words that describe what you really mean, and you'll be well on the way to developing your 'author voice'.

It ain't what you say . . .

Of course it's not just *what* you write, but what you write *about* that defines you as an author. Knowing what to expect from Catherine Cookson, or Jane Austen, has less to do with their style than their subject matter.

Why is Thomas Hardy considered a great poet, for example? His verse is sometimes twee to the point of being cringe-worthy; he contorts syllables and uses outrageous archaisms in the cause of rhythm and rhyme.

Thy shadow, earth, from pole to central sea,
Now steals along the moon's meek shine,
In even monochrome and curving line
Of imperturbable serenity.

So far, so 'Hallmark' greetings card if you ask me. If that was all there was to Hardy then the big cheeses of twentieth-century English poetry (people like Philip Larkin for example) would hardly have given him a second glance. But then, in verse two things start getting serious:

How shall I link such sun-cast symmetry
With the torn-troubled form I know as thine,
That profile, placid as a brow divine,
With continents of moil and misery?

Now we're into Hardy territory. Watching a rare lunar eclipse he not only wants to record the experience, but examine his own emotional response and then to put humanity with all its self-importance firmly in its place. And so, in the final verse, we get:

Is such the stellar gauge of earthly show?
Nation at war with nation, brains that teem,
Heroes, and women fairer than the skies.

Suddenly we're at a new and exciting place – and those final lines pretty well sum up Hardy's subject matter, whether as a novelist or a poet: conflict, brains that teem, heroes . . . and of course, women 'fairer than the skies'.

And that – more than anything else – is what makes Hardy a great writer. Not only does he have a consistency of subject-matter over a lifetime's work as a novelist and poet, his subjects are the big ones: life, death and of course, love.

Exercise 2.4

What kinds of subjects interest you, both as a reader and a writer? Have you got a particular world view you want to share with your readers? What – if anything – would you hope someone reading your work would take from it?

What's it all about?

Lastly, of course, comes the question of why you write, what you want to write and what you like to read. This is what is sometimes referred to as an author's 'poetics' and I suppose it's a bit like a brief literary biography, detailing a writer's authorly relations and ambitions as well as their 'theory' of literature in general.

Don't be put off by this, and don't dismiss it either. Taking a moment to think about precisely why you write what you write, what you hope to achieve, why anyone writes and what writing is for is a useful discipline. Many 'writers' (myself included) tend to write first, think afterwards without first having a clear understanding of what it is they're doing. Well, mystery tours can sometimes be quite interesting; but you can also end up hopelessly lost.

Think of this final exercise as your author-manifesto, make it as detailed as you can and share it with any would-be writers that you know. That way they will begin to know a little bit more about you as a writer, and you will have a clearer idea of where you're going with your writing. And knowing your destination is no bad thing at the start of any journey.

Exercise 2.5

Write your own 'poetics' now. What do you think literature is for? Why do you want to be a writer? What experience has brought you to where you are now, and what purpose do you intend your creative work to serve?

Summing Up

▦ Reading as a writer is vitally important. But so is knowing why you choose to read the books you read and reading them critically – as an author.

▦ Although clichés and commonly-used expressions can be useful, we owe it to our readers to attempt to be original.

▦ What you say, as a writer, is as important in the development of your own unique 'voice' as the way you say it. And you should have a clear idea of what you think your writing is for, as well as where it's going.

Chapter Three

Reading as a Writer

This chapter builds on the work done in the previous chapter and develops the idea of reading critically with a writer's eye. What makes a successful book, and can you see 'behind the scenes' and find out how it's done?

Reading for writing is not the same as editing. We'll be talking about editing and proof-reading in a later chapter. But before ever putting pen to paper, a writer needs to cultivate the same critical faculties as film directors have when watching other people's movies, or car mechanics driving other people's cars or gardeners in other people's gardens. You can admire what you're looking at, but you also need to start instinctively asking questions about it, learning from it, and making judgements about it.

For an author this means asking questions like:

* Why was this book enjoyable?

* How does the author keep my interest?

* What would happen if one or two words in that paragraph were changed?

* Why does the rhythm of a particular sentence flow so smoothly?

And so on.

Opening time

Developing this kind of critical eye takes time, but learning to do it can be fun. Here are a few games you can play to get into the mood, so-to-speak . . .

'If there is something necessary to all writing it is, I believe, to read like crazy. Read everything you can in whichever genre you are pursuing. Read old works and new and let it all sink into you. None of us can write in a vacuum.'

Sue Guiney, novelist and playwright

Exercise 3.1

Choose one of your favourite books; read the opening sentences a couple of times carefully. What (if anything) about the passage makes you want to read on? Is there anything about the words you'd like to change? Could the writing be improved?

'I love the work of Jane Smiley and Ann Patchett. Also Marilynne Robinson. What all these have in common is an honesty of voice and attention to the beauty of language.'

Sue Guiney, novelist and playwright

Thinking critically about a good book isn't the same as being critical of it, or the author. Just because you're starting out you needn't feel reticent about questioning the 'greats'. It's an imperfect world and even the best books contain bad writing. If you're serious about your own writing then your antennae should be twitching every time you read anything, from the morning 'paper to the Booker winner. Admire the greats, by all means, but go beyond mere admiration: why does what you're reading 'work', and what – if anything – could be improved? Thinking like this not only trains your writer's eye, but has the added advantage of making clear that no work of literature is ever faultless, a fact that can be remarkably encouraging to the would-be writer.

Exercise 3.2

Here are a few more opening passages, all taken from well-known novels. If you were browsing in a bookshop, which one would tempt you to read on and why?

i. No one who had ever seen Catherine Morland in her infancy would have supposed her to have been born an heroine.

ii. Happy families are all alike; every unhappy family is unhappy in its own way.

iii. It was the best of times, it was the worst of times, it was the age of wisdom, it was the age of foolishness, it was the epoch of belief, it was the epoch of incredulity, it was the season of Light, it was the season of Darkness, it was the spring of hope, it was the winter of despair.

iv. Call me Ishmael.

v. This is not a real book; not really.

vi. You don't know about me without you have read a book by the name of The Adventures of Tom Sawyer; but that ain't no matter.

vii. I wish either my father or my mother, or indeed both of them, as they were in duty both equally bound to it, had minded what they were about when they begot me . . .

viii. Whether I shall turn out to be the hero of my own life, or whether that station will be held by anybody else, these pages must show.

ix. For a long time, I went to bed early.

x. I was born in the Year 1632, in the City of York, of a good Family, tho' not of that Country, my Father being a Foreigner of Bremen, who settled first at Hull . . .

The Meat in the sandwich

Of course, once you've caught the reader's interest you have to work hard to maintain it. The story, the setting, the characterisation, dialogue and explanation all have to pull together in order to ensure the pages keep on being turned. How do the authors you admire do that?

If you're not careful this can begin to turn into literary criticism, which is not the purpose of this chapter. Book reviews, magazine articles and academic treatises on an author or a book don't really tell you what a writer needs to know. What you need to do is mentally de-construct the book, search for the joins, see how it's done and learn from what's been written – none of which is easy.

Thankfully, there are a number of things you can do to help make such 'mental undressing' a little more straightforward. To begin with you can simply pick up a book you admire and go looking for clues. What makes the experience of reading enjoyable? Why is the story so satisfying? What is it about the author's style that you enjoy? If an entire book seems daunting, take a sample passage and examine it in detail. And examine it with a purpose. One way to do this is to re-write the passage, making deliberate changes 'for better or worse' (as the Prayer Book says about a slightly different subject matter).

'Once you've caught the reader's interest you have to work hard to maintain it.'

Exercise 3.3

Take a favourite passage from a book: any book, any genre, published or unpublished, your own, someone else's, finished or a work-in-progress. First, go through the passage asking yourself the kind of questions listed above. If it's a piece of your own work, be as ruthless and dispassionate as possible.

Next, the fun part. Re-write the passage a couple of times, making deliberate changes. You could insert adverbs, change the sex or name of the protagonist(s), change the setting, alter the tense, change the perspective (e.g. first to third person) – anything. Enjoy this, and be as outrageous as you can!

Here's an extract from my novel, Writing Therapy*, as an example. First, the original:

'Who's your captain?' somebody was saying.

'I am,' Ted replied.

'Ok, then – heads or tails?'

Ted lost. We fielded first. Or rather, most of us just stood around and waited for the ball to come in our direction. Fielding implies a certain dynamism which was sadly lacking in our team's efforts. Lizzie, for a start, kept running in the wrong direction. Now, there are studies suggesting anorexics have a problem with basic navigation. Back then it was just another source of irritation.

'Lizzie – watch the ball!' Ted shouted as she missed another catch.

The rehab team were good. They enjoyed Ted's bowling, hitting him so far that sometimes they were able to complete a double rounder, or whatever.

'Thirty-nine to win then,' Mrs Lotinga was trilling as we lined up to take our turn at batting.

Ted went first, and scored a couple before holing out to someone in the deep. The rehab team could catch. I went in next. I thought I did ok. I scored a few more – so did everybody, even Lizzie. But gradually we began to fall away, either run-out, caught or – in the case of Debbie – missing the ball completely.

Jane was last in. Three more needed, and some tricky bowling still to come. She set herself, then whacked the ball and started running. Ted was screaming, but Jane wasn't awfully athletic. A fielder in the deep was returning the ball just as she set off from the penultimate base. With a flourish the fielder at fourth base collected the ball and demolished the post.

'Oh bad luck Jane,' Sophie shouted. 'Yeah, well tried!' we echoed.

All that is, except for Ted. He stormed off the field, marching straight back to the adolescent unit, missing the post-match party.

'I remember that,' said Sophie.

'It was quite amusing, really. And, do you remember how – once he'd gone – we started talking about him?'

'Someone said how childish his behaviour was.'

Yes, we all joined in, including Jane.'

'All,' I said, 'except for Monica.'

Monica had been listening.

'Michael Ondaatje is probably the author I find most consistently satisfying. He has a lyrical, poetic way of telling a story that I truly adore and envy. Finishing in Ondaatje novel is like waking from a dream.'
Gary William Murning, novelist

Now, here's the same passage having made a few changes:

When we arrived, somebody asked who our team's captain was. Ted, of course, immediately said it was him before anyone else had a chance to speak, just like he lost the toss and announced that he would be our bowler.

That meant we all had to stand around and wait for the ball to come in our direction, which was something else that annoyed Ted. You couldn't really call it fielding. 'Fielding' implies a certain dynamism which was sadly lacking in our team's efforts. Lizzie, for example, just kept running in the wrong direction. There have been studies suggesting anorexics have a problem with basic navigation. Back then it was just another source of irritation and Ted kept shouting at her as she ran the wrong way for a catch.

The rehab team were good. They enjoyed Ted's bowling, hitting him so far that sometimes they were able to complete a double rounder, or whatever it's called. By the end of their innings they'd scored thirty-eight, which gave us a target of thirty-nine.

Ted batted first, and scored a couple before holing out to someone in the deep. The rehab team could catch. I went in next. I thought I did ok. I scored a few more – so did everybody, even Lizzie. But gradually we began to fall away, either run-out, caught or – in the case of Debbie – missing the ball completely.

Jane was last in. Three more needed, and some tricky bowling still to come. She set herself, then whacked the ball and started running. Ted was screaming, but Jane wasn't awfully athletic. A fielder in the deep was returning the ball just as she set off from the penultimate post. With a flourish the fielder at fourth base collected the ball and demolished the post.

'Oh bad luck Jane,' Sophie shouted. 'Yeah, well tried!' we echoed.

All that is, except for Ted. He stormed off the field, marching straight back to the adolescent unit, missing the post-match party. It was quite amusing, really. Once he'd gone we started talking about him. Someone said how childish his behaviour was. We all joined in, including Jane.

All, that is, except for Monica.

Before anyone gets the wrong idea I should point out that I've chosen a passage from one of my books for two simple reasons: one, I own the copyright and can therefore quote extensively and two, I already have a ready-made 're-write' of that passage, so I suppose I'm cheating!

Which version works 'best' depends on a number of different factors, but the first, with dialogue – 'showing' rather than telling – would generally be regarded as superior. Personally, I quite like the alternative narrative passage and I'm glad I didn't delete it. But it shows how different the same thing can be, and this is an exercise you should try and repeat several times with different passages, changing different things each time.

'Max Hastings, Simon Sebag Montefiore – readable riveting prose. Clive James for being unbelievably funny: 'the Trekkies have landed on a planet that looks exactly like a set. Appropriately enough it is peopled entirely by bad actors'. Fantastic.'

Guy de la Bédoyère, author and historian

Summing Up

- Reading for writing starts when you begin to ask questions like 'why does this passage work?' and 'what would happen if it was changed?'

- You can practise reading for writing in a number of ways, including 're-writing' passages of well-known works.

- Even the best writers' work can sometimes be improved.

Chapter Four

Fact and Fiction

- *Where does fact end and fiction begin?*
- *How are the two genres related and can you be good at writing both?*
- *What makes good writing 'true'?*

'There's no such thing as fiction, only fact gone wrong . . . .'

An extreme view perhaps, but the dividing line between fact and fiction is never clear, and fiction writers are notorious for raiding their own (and other people's) lives for the sake of a good story. This chapter, I suppose, is as much about inspiration as about different types of writing, which is appropriate when you consider the fact that the differences between the two are often only superficial.

The truth, the whole truth . . .

Many great works of fiction have been thinly disguised fact, and many a so-called true story has been embellished to the point of becoming more fantasy than reality. Consider George Orwell's classic *Animal Farm*. On the face of it, it's a book about farmyard animals taking over a farm, but of course it's also much more than that and is in fact a thinly disguised account of the Russian revolution and its aftermath. One of the first 'novels' (if not *the* first) ever written – *Robinson Crusoe* – was thought to have been based on the real-life experience of one Henry Pitman, sometime surgeon and Monmouth rebel.

To illustrate the close connections between fact and fiction, try this short exercise in both.

'Many great works of fiction have been thinly disguised fact, and many a so-called true story has been embellished to the point of becoming more fantasy than reality.'

> ## Exercise 4.1
>
> Think of a real character from your own life: a relative or friend, but someone with a strong personality about whom plenty can be written. Now write a mini biography (the kind of thing you see in concert programmes, or on the back of books). Next consider what you would have to do to fictionalise it – change the names, perhaps, and other telling details while retaining the arc of the biography. Then write it out a second time as if it were a work of fiction.

'Everything that happens in my novels tends to come from, as I believe it should, how the characters react to a given set of circumstances. Yes, there may be a central 'event' that gets the ball rolling, but, at heart, the story grows from how the characters deal with this.'

Gary William Murning, novelist

Tell all the truth, but tell it slant . . .

Because there never was (and probably never will be) a farm in which the animals turned on their human masters, can *Animal Farm* be true? If a story hasn't happened in reality, is it a lie? Without getting too philosophical here, we need to consider briefly the relationship between truth and fiction and establish a couple of basic rules.

Any parent reading fairy tales to their children (or even watching certain children's television programmes) can't fail to be aware of the 'messages' such stories contain. It doesn't really matter if there really was a boy who cried wolf: the truth of the tale is universal. Good literature is just like this: it tells us something true about human nature irrespective of the factual details of the story. *King Lear* (indeed, most of Shakespeare) might say more about the workings of the human mind than an entire library of psychological case studies. The vanities, jealousies, struggles, triumphs and disasters are all there and they pass through the generations like the words in a stick of seaside rock. Good fiction holds a mirror to these truths, and thus is always 'true' – but in a very different way to factual writing.

Non-fiction – to the extent that it is worth reading – seeks to do a similar kind of thing. Whether it is history, biography, autobiography or literary analysis, good non-fiction writing involves teasing out the universal truths of the human condition and showing them in a particular setting.

Need2Know

Exercise 4.2

Think of an incident from your own life – or the life of someone close to you – that was typical in some way of the experience of almost everyone. Maybe a first experience of love and loss; a time when pride came before a fall; a solemn warning that went unheeded (but proved to be accurate); a sacrifice made for the good of someone else.

Write this incident up as if it had happened to someone else – either a well-known character from fiction (books or television) or somebody known to you. Try writing it in the third person ('She knew when she woke up that something was wrong') as a way of further distancing yourself from the experience, but don't worry if this proves difficult. Be aware of what the moral of the story is supposed to be, and remain true to that.

The devil is in the detail

Without straying far from the theme of this chapter, it'd be worth considering for a moment what it takes to make a character in a piece of writing – any writing, fact or fiction – seem 'real' to the reader. If you were an historian and you wanted to capture the essence of a great historical figure, or a biographer keen to bring alive the subject of your biography, or a novelist desperate to make your characters come alive, what is it that you would have to do?

The answer is surprisingly similar in all three cases. There's no 'magic wand' to be waved which makes a character – fictional or real – come alive on the page, but there are one or two tricks to be learnt which can help pull the rabbit from the hat.

> 'Just as in real life, a saggy middle can be a real turn-off.'
>
> Tamsyn Murray, author of *My So-Called Afterlife*

'There's no 'magic wand' to be waved which makes a character – fictional or real – come alive on the page, but there are one or two tricks to be learnt which can help pull the rabbit from the hat.'

This is the kind of thing writers do all the time. Of course, if you're dealing with a real person the 'facts' will already be available. But presenting them in such a format can reveal a few surprises. For a fictional character, such details might not ever feature in the narrative you're creating. But knowing them means that your writing will be more convincing.

Taking shape

In fiction, of course, things happen in a particular way for the sake of a satisfying story. Real-life seldom presents us with a logical narrative sequence that can be transferred directly to the page. The art of great story-telling (whether in a novel or a work of history or biography) is to keep the reader's or listener's interest – which means giving shape and structure to a story.

Little has changed in this regard for thousands of years. The early Greek epics, the Norse Sagas, early Romances and the first novels all tend to follow a very simple three act narrative structure:

- Set up.

- Confrontation.

- Resolution

Exercise 4.4

Go back through a couple of books you've recently finished reading and see if you can make them fit this three-act structure. Is it easy or difficult, and what does that say about the quality of the book you've chosen?

Of course there are a thousand different ways of doing this, which is why there are so many good books on the market. We'll examine plot and structure in more detail in a later chapter, but for now it is enough to appreciate that – whatever form of writing you're engaged in – you need to tell a story, fact or fiction, in a structured way.

Writing non-fiction

Non-fiction is often regarded as a specialist area, different to fiction and produced by a different type of author. To a certain extent, of course, this is true. But as I hope I've already argued:

- The dividing line between fact and fiction is not as clear as we sometimes think.

- A great many fiction writers also write excellent non-fiction, whether in the form of travel writing (think Ernest Hemingway) autobiography or even history.

Again, I'll be taking a detailed look at non-fiction a little later in this book. For now be aware that for the would-be author the boundary between the two areas of writing is both unnecessary and artificial. Each of us, as we learn the craft of writing, needs to practise doing both. As Bill Herbert, Professor of Poetry and Creative Writing at Newcastle University, puts it:

'Don't determine what you are before you've an inkling as to who you are. Lots of writers decide far too fast that they're a poet or prose writer or dramatist, then use it as a means of limiting and controlling their creativity – they stop reading novels, 'hate' opera or football, won't attend poetry readings, have endless 'opinions'. The one thing creativity is never about is closing yourself off like this – the one thing you definitely don't know is where your next idea is coming from.'

(Interview with the author, November 2011)

Looking ahead

The traditional image of the writer eking out a solitary existence in his artistic garret is probably a bit extreme. On the other hand, writing is often a solitary activity. If you're fortunate enough to know instinctively what readers want to read (without ever asking their opinion) you're about to make a fortune. The rest of us often need a friendly pair of eyes to look at what we've written and to make suggestions. If you've already found someone to do this for you, that's excellent. Just make sure they're able to give the kind of feedback that you need. If not, now's the time to start looking. As you proceed through this book, sharing some of the things you learn and the words you write with someone else will become increasingly important.

Summing Up

- The dividing line between fact and fiction is often thinner than we realise, and most writers plunder real-life for their stories.

- Just because something hasn't happened, doesn't mean it isn't true. One of the great purposes of fiction is to reveal universal truths about the human condition, a purpose often achieved more easily through a cast of fictional characters.

- Character creation – whether real or imagined – is the central task of any prose writer and can be helped by considering a wide range of details, many of which will never figure in the finished manuscript.

- All stories have a structure: real-life must be edited to fit, and fiction must present the reader with a satisfying narrative to keep the pages turning.

Chapter Five

Verse and Worse

- *Does a poem have to rhyme?*
- *How do you detect the rhythm in a poem?*
- *What makes a poem different from prose and what use is poetry to the committed prose writer?*

Of all the chapters in this book, this is probably the most specialist. Poetry can be a bit of a Marmite area and even those of us who like it, write it and are otherwise 'into' it often have strong views and can be very defensive about them. Take the first question (above) – does a poem have to rhyme? For some people, that's everything: no rhyme = no poem. But Shakespeare didn't rhyme; not all the time. So what actually makes poetry different from prose?

The rhythm of life

What's the difference between the following sentences?

- The boy stood on the burning deck
- The boy was standing on the burning deck
- The deck around where the boy was standing was burning

Ok, too easy. But useful, I hope. Of course, all three sentences have rhythm: every sentence does, to some degree. But the first (the one that everyone knows) has a regular beat and a forward momentum which is usually the mark of good poetry. (I'm not saying, necessarily, that *Casabianca* is a great poem, or that Felicia Dorothea Hemans was a great poet although – incidentally – her *Landing of the Pilgrim Fathers in New England* has assumed the status almost of a sacred text in the USA, despite her never having been there!)

> 'Poetry can be a bit of a Marmite area and even those of us who like it, write it and are otherwise 'into' it often have strong views and can be very defensive about them.'

Let's look at that first line again:

The BOY stood ON the BURNing DECK

There is a fairly clear four-stress rhythm in that line; the next line:

Whence ALL but HE had FLED

. . . has only three stresses, and you'll notice that each 'dum' (what we poets *ahem* call a 'foot') is preceded by an unstressed syllable (a'de').

This is called ballad metre (or Common Metre, abbreviated C.M. in things like hymn books) and is the 'de-dum, de-dum, de-dum, de-dum' pattern that almost everybody recognises.

Technically, we could say that the first line of *Casiabanca* is an iambic tetrameter and the second, an iambic trimeter and that the rhyming pattern is A-B-A-B but we won't. I think we'll leave that to the advanced guide. If there is one.

The point is that there is a deliberate – and memorable – rhythm to the line which is part of its appeal. Arranging words in order – whether as a poet or a prose writer – is more than a matter of merely transmitting information. Rearranging or changing words (as I did, above) can subtly alter the rhythm of a sentence and make it more or less effective.

Rhyme time

Actually, that sub-heading is rather misleading. The subject of rhyme and its many variations would take an entire book to cover adequately. Suffice to say that words rhyme in a variety of ways (some of which aren't considered 'proper' by poetry purists) but the simple reason for getting words to rhyme is this: so that you can remember them. Rhyming dates from a time when all literature was transmitted orally and it was necessary in order to make large tracts of writing easier to remember. It's been used as a teaching tool for thousands of years, which is why many religious works seem to have echoes (if not overt traces) of the poetry they once were.

Exercise 5.1

To reinforce this message, have a go at rearranging the following lines (re-written – badly – from well-known poems) into more memorably rhythmical lines. You never know, you might even end up with the original line as written by the poet!

1. I earn money by day, and drink a lot at night

2. Stop the clocks then turn off the telephone

3. When a criminal's not engaged in illegal activity

4. My girl, she's like a lovely flower

5. I met my love next to the salley gardens

6. What bell tolls for these who go to their deaths like cattle?

7. It is midnight, and I'm imagining a forest

8. Don't tell me here, it doesn't need to be said

9. I know somewhere where wild thyme blows

10. Can you stay cool when all the other dudes are bricking it?

Of course, the fact that we can now commit words to paper and have little need for rote learning isn't the only reason rhyme has come to be seen as less than essential in poetry, but it is undoubtedly a factor. As we've seen, the rhythm of a sentence is a vitally important element in poetry, and can easily supplant the need for rhyme. But together, they're a powerful combination and worthy of examination.

Exercise 5.2

Try rhyming the following words: car; tree; red; box; ice; flower; moaning; windmill; railway; service.

'Rhyming dates from a time when all literature was transmitted orally and it was necessary in order to make large tracts of writing easier to remember. It's been used as a teaching tool for thousands of years.'

Even a simple task like that should reveal one important detail about rhyme: single syllables are (generally) easier than multiples, and if you can only rhyme the last syllable of any of the polysyllabic words, you're guilty of a half-rhyme. But does any of that matter?

Are you free?

Poetry, verse, call it what you will now comes in lots of different shapes and sizes. The rhythm of the words is vital, but the rhyme can sometimes be dispensed with. When it is, it's often referred to as either 'blank' or 'free verse' for the simple reason that it's free of rhyme.

It's at this point that we're as near as we're going to get to answering the last of this chapter's three questions: what's the difference between poetry and prose, and is the former any use to prose writers? And to answer it, I'm going to quote a short passage from a book by Roger Deakin, *Waterlog*:

The restless Dorset sea fondles and gropes
at the rock-shelf like a lover's hand
up a stockinged thigh . . .
The snowy waves shampoo over the rocks
And waterfall off its seaward rim.

> ### Exercise 5.3
>
> The $64,000 question is this: is that extract poetry or prose?
>
> Before reading on, consider your own answer. Decide what you think it is and consider the reasons for your decision.

I wonder what you decided and why, and if you'd be surprised to learn that – whatever your choice – you're probably right. Rather unfairly, I arranged the lines on the page to look like poetry, but they're actually from a work written entirely in prose.

> **Poetry, verse, call it what you will now comes in lots of different shapes and sizes.**

But revealingly, the late Roger Deakin once admitted in an interview that his writing notes were often written in the form of poetry. Not, perhaps, the 'de-dum, de-dum, de-dum' poetry of *Casiabanca*, still less the kind of poetry that rhymes obviously – but poetry, nevertheless. The words pass themselves off quite convincingly as verse, not just because they may once have been written that way, but because of the intense, poetic focus of the imagery and the almost luxuriant use of simile. It's far more concentrated than you'd normally get in prose, and an entire book written like that might be a tad indigestible. But as a way of sketching – quickly – a situation and recording as much information as possible, poetry is a handy addition to any prose writer's tool kit.

Exercise 5.4

Try writing your own short poem now. Maybe you're already working on a prose project (either fact or fiction). If so, you could use it as a way of quickly 'sketching' a forthcoming scene, trying to convey as much sensory information in as few words as you can. Or perhaps you'd simply like to write a poem for poetry's sake – there's no better motivation.

Decide on your subject and imagine it. You could 'brainstorm' or 'list' as many words as you associate with this act of imagining before crafting them into verse form. Remember, as Philip Larkin once said, your chief responsibility is to the experience itself. You want to convey what it's like to be there, to see it, feel it, touch it, smell it, to the reader: really bring it alive for them.

Poetry is intensely personal, and if you aren't sure you want to share it with anyone I'm sure no-one will be offended. But if you do, let it go: see if other people 'get' it, and if they do, then you're launched on a career in poetry.

Summing Up

- Poems don't have to rhyme, but all poems must at least have a recognisable rhythm;

- The stronger the rhythm (of whatever pattern) the better, generally, the poem;

- In some ways, poetry is like prose, distilled. Its focus can be a useful tool for any writer.

Chapter Six

The Novel

In this chapter we take a closer look at fiction, examining different styles and genres and the question of sustained writing.

- *What is a 'novel' and how long has the form been around?*

- *What are the different types of fiction and how strong are the boundaries?*

- *How is a novel constructed?*

- *How do I start writing a novel, and what's the secret of sustained writing?*

In the grand scheme of things, the sustained work of prose fiction – or 'novel' as we now know it – hasn't been around for very long. Until approximately 250 years ago if you wanted fiction, you either went to the theatre or listened to a bard recite one of the epic poems (that is, if you were of a Lordly disposition) or else heard someone sing a ballad. And there was one very good reason for that – most people couldn't read and if they could, they'd be reading things like the Bible. There wasn't much else available.

The first novel in English is generally thought to be *Robinson Crusoe*, by Daniel Defoe. Of course, that depends how you define a 'novel' and as that's the subject of this particular chapter, it's an apposite place to begin thinking.

'Until approximately 250 years ago if you wanted fiction, you either went to the theatre or listened to a bard recite one of the epic poems.'

Exercise 6.1

What is a novel? What makes a novel different from other works of literature, and how do you know when you're reading a novel? Try making a list of some of the common characteristics of the novels you read, and then see if you can find an example that doesn't tick all the boxes.

Does it have to be in prose? Does it have to be entirely fictional? How long does a novel have to be? These aren't easy questions, but most critics generally think that a novel should be almost entirely prose and almost entirely fictional. This, then, excludes the re-telling of an epic like *La Morte d'Arthur* (1485) and all of Chaucer (which would otherwise knock *Crusoe* off his perch). And let's not forget that we're talking here about the *English* novel: Italian Giovanni Boccaccio's book, *The Decameron* (which seems to have influenced Chaucer) dates from as early as 1353.

As for length, a novel is usually more than 50,000 words long and can be anything up to 150,000 words or more. The 'average' (such as it is) varies for different genres of fiction, but is usually thought to be around 80,000 words.

Genres

Humans seem to like things to be stored away in neat categories. Ever since Adam was given the job of naming all the animals in *Genesis*, we've been making lists and inventing classifications. Books are no different. There are horror stories, romances, erotic fiction, chick lit, the historical novel, science fiction, lad lit and literary fiction to name just a few. And you don't have to analyse your own reading habits to see where your preference lies: just look at the back cover of the books you're reading and you'll find a helpful little label designed to help the book shop or the library put it on the right shelf.

Is any of this important? Well, yes. Some genres have their own conventions and while it's perfectly acceptable to push the boundaries, if you're writing a thriller and you don't at least know the kind of shorthand references or genre clichés that are popular, you're at a disadvantage. So it's worth thinking about the type of book you're writing, not because you want it to be like all the other books in that particular genre, but so that you have a clear idea what readers of books like yours want to read. There'll be more about each of the different genres in a later chapter. But in the meantime, if you're not sure what kind of book you're writing call it 'literary' fiction. No-one's ever going to contradict you!

Nuts and Bolts

Although they're all different (or should be: they're not called 'novels' for nothing!) most books share certain common features which are regarded pretty much as essential for their success. This doesn't mean that all successful books are built the same way, as anyone who's ever tried reading *Ulysses* will appreciate. But the following elements are useful to consider even if you plan a grand literary gesture.

Structure

Read ten different novels and – if you're choosing carefully – you could find ten different types of structure, which isn't very helpful if you're learning the craft. Writers and tutors often refer to the 'arc' of the story, which in its simplest form is:

- Set up.
- Confrontation.
- Resolution.

Basically, if you're writing a novel (as opposed to, say, a short story) you've got to take the reader on a bit of a holiday: short stories are away-days; novels are the full vacation and *War and Peace* is the year-long round-the-world cruise. Which means there's got to be plenty going on: there will be sub-plots, apparent solutions (which turn out to be anything but) and real emotional and psychological development.

And don't forget the three act structure doesn't have to happen in that order: some books (and not a few films) start the action at the final destination and then reveal how the characters arrived there as part of the story. Or you could open with a confrontation and follow with the set up, or the background information. Whatever you do, remember your story can't just 'happen'. You have to craft it into a satisfying piece of entertainment, which will mean teasing the reader a little. No-one pays to see a strip-tease if it doesn't: an author needs to know what to reveal and when, and only get his or her kit off (as it were) in the final chapter!

'Basically, if you're writing a novel (as opposed to, say, a short story) you've got to take the reader on a bit of a holiday: short stories are away-days; novels are the full vacation and War and Peace is the year-long round-the-world cruise.'

Exercise 6.2

Consider this for a moment. Were you one of the children in the playground who could command the attention of a great gaggle of friends as you regaled them with a tale of what happened at the weekend? It's the skill all great after-dinner speakers have to develop. How to transform 'events' into a story.

Have a go at this now. Think of something – anything – that's happened to you recently (preferably something out of the ordinary) and craft it as an anecdote or story. Make the best of it – decide what the 'punch-line' is going to be and determine the most entertaining way of getting there.

Perspective

First person, second person, third person? For most novels it's either the former or the latter. Sometimes it's a combination of the two. Rarely – but interestingly – a novel will be written in the second person: 'You hated Spain; you said it would be fine but for the Spaniards'. Your choice of perspective depends on the kind of story you're trying to tell. If you really want to get in the central character's skin, first person might be the way to go. You can decide if you want the narrator to be reliable or not according to the story that you're telling. For example, if you're writing about childhood infatuation, telling the story directly via an obviously delusional narrator might be an effective strategy. On the other hand, a third person narrator might be able to tell the reader things about the central character which even they don't know. This kind of all-knowing (or 'omniscient') narration is probably most common.

Description

Without turning on the purple prose, every author needs to think carefully about descriptive passages. On a blog post a while ago I played a game of 'choose ten books a writer ought to read' and one was a 'Windsor and Newton' watercolour pad. I was only half-joking. To describe anything, you've got to look and look again. Don't glance, then glance away and immediately begin writing. Doing that will almost certainly lead to the kind of clichéd descriptions any second-rate author could have penned. But you're not that author. So look hard, and really 'see'.

Of course, certain similes and metaphors seem to lend themselves to descriptive prose: as smooth as silk; as happy as a sand-boy; calm as a mill-pond. But what marks a really creative writer is choosing some new and exciting comparison: something that makes the reader sit up and think 'yes – I'd never noticed that before or thought about it in that way, but that's true!' Try to make your descriptive prose informative and original.

Characterisation

Perhaps the most important element in the novel is the presentation and development of the protagonists – in other words, characterisation. Bringing a character to life and presenting them as somebody engaging and memorable is the real magic of the novel. It brings together the previous three elements and quite simply makes or breaks the story. I remember an early editor's report on my own novel in which a reader had said of my narrator: 'on page 102 she tries to kill herself and – to be blunt – I rather wish that she'd succeeded.' Oh dear . . .

Of course you can't please all the people all the time. One reason I don't read much romantic fiction is that I find it hard to identify – still less, sympathise – with the characters. But whether they're good or bad, float everybody's boat or leave them wanting less, your characters must be strong. There's really only one trick to make characters strong: to know everything about them. Everything: what colour pants they're wearing, whether they prefer dogs to cats, like Marmite, eat with their fingers while watching the telly and have a secret obsession with Australian cricketers. And let's be clear about this: just because you know it, doesn't mean it's going in the book. But because you know it, what does go in the book will be a great deal more convincing.

> 'Before writing, before even beginning to outline a novel, I will often carry the central characters for it around in my head for 6 to 12 months – getting to know them, listening to them speak, learning about their individual stories.'
>
> Gary William Murning, novelist

Exercise 6.3

It's great fun inventing characters, but we all need a place to start. Although we'll almost inevitably base aspects of a character on some real-life examples, as a starting point basing a character on a real person is a dangerous game and likely to end up in court. So take a picture from a magazine or newspaper – ads are the best examples as, in many cases, we don't know who the person is – and use it as a basis for character creation. You've got the basic physical information. But what else are you going to say about this person?

Carry on . . . Writing

Ok, so you've started. Believe it or not, that's the easy bit. Now you've got to carry on. Sustaining a work of fiction for 50, 60, 70 or 80,000 words is a feat of endurance and if you're finding it hard to keep going there could be a number of reasons. Are you finding it interesting? If not, give up; neither will your readers. Are you blocked? If so, just write; write gobbledegook; write rubbish; just write *something*.

Most writers find starting again after a break a little difficult. Many suggest leaving the story at a point at which you know what's going to happen next; that way, you'll have an easy start next time. I've even heard of writers who stop mid-sentence. Little tricks like that can make it easier to pick up the next day.

You'll notice there are slightly fewer writing exercises in this chapter. There are two reasons for that. First, I hope you're already actively working on something that you intend to submit for publication. We'll talk in more detail about that at a later stage. Second, you can make an exercise out of any one of the sections in this chapter and I'd rather you did.

I hope something has struck a chord in relation to your own work. Rather than be led by things marked 'exercise' I hope you'll be able to take some of the material as the starting point for doing something we'll be looking at more closely in the next section: editing your work.

'Most writers find starting again after a break a little difficult. Many suggest leaving the story at a point at which you know what's going to happen next; that way, you'll have an easy start next time.'

Summing Up

■ The novel as an art form is relatively new and is evolving all the time; there are boundaries and common elements and themes, but be prepared to break the mould;

■ If you are planning something new, know which mould you're breaking. Genres are convenient pigeon-holes but they exist for a reason. At the very least, they can tell you what a group of readers enjoy reading;

■ Of all the bits that go to make up a good novel, characterisation is the most important. Just as you might expect to know your best friend or partner intimately, make sure you know everything about your central character;

■ Writing a novel is like running a marathon: you're going to hit a wall somewhere; write through it, and there are a number of tricks you can use to help you.

Chapter Seven

Be Your Own Editor

Any form of writing should be the best that you can make it before considering submitting to editors, publishers, agents etc. In this chapter you'll learn how to examine your own work critically and dispassionately.

What is an editor, and what do they do? No doubt a great many authors have a positive relationship with a tactful but perceptive editor who sees it as his or her gentle duty to act as midwife to the birth of a new literary masterpiece. But there are others who appear to think their job is more important than that of the author. If you're lucky and you land someone in the former category, you're home and dry; if not, and your work crosses the desk of someone struggling with too many authors in too many different genres, you'll be thankful that you spent time editing, re-editing and editing again yourself before you submitted. And that's not easy.

But it is essential.

Exercise 7.1

Imagine the Rev'd W. Awdry has just delivered the latest 'Thomas' epic to your office. As editor, what would you do with the following lines?

'Thomas loved taking the children in his carriages. He rushed off as quickly as he could to the station. He arrived at the station in no time. The children were all waiting for him at the station. They cheered when they saw him arrive.'

Of course, there's nothing exactly *wrong* with what the Rev'd Awdry has written. Not as such. But wouldn't the following be a little more, well . . . interesting?

'If your work crosses the desk of someone struggling with too many authors in too many different genres, you'll be thankful that you spent time editing, re-editing and editing again yourself before you submitted.'

'Thomas loved taking the children in his carriages, so he hurried as quickly as he could to the station. He got there in no time and the children cheered the moment they saw him arrive.'

Simple, but effective – and in many ways that's what an editor is there to do – to iron out the creases; ensure the story flows; make sure that there's consistency between each section of the book (e.g. that the central character doesn't suddenly lose three years in age between chapters one and ten). And you *can* do it all for yourself – perhaps not as well as a professional editor, but well enough to make your eventual discussions with one more productive and rewarding for you both.

Step away from the computer

The first thing you need to do – and this is not an option – is forget about your work, put that book away, hide the poem in a drawer, bury that story or article under a pile of laundry and go about your day to day business. Do something else; anything – writing, reading, rock-climbing if you so choose. But don't even think about getting out that *magnum opus*. Leave it. Let it grow.

'Your first draft is a bit like a seed, and committing it to paper is like planting it in fertile soil. You water it, of course; but then you leave it. You don't pull it up at the first sign of green shoots to see how it's doing.

> **'Your first draft is a bit like a seed, and committing it to paper is like planting it in fertile soil. You water it, of course; but then you leave it. You don't pull it up at the first sign of green shoots to see how it's doing.'**

Exercise 7.2

Of course, in the heat of the creative moment it can be difficult to leave a piece of creative writing, especially when you know that it needs more work. Perhaps you've already got a long-neglected piece of writing mouldering in a drawer somewhere or hidden in a long-forgotten folder on your computer? Dig it out now, and read it afresh; what changes would you make as your own editor? It should be a lot easier to see what needs doing after distancing yourself from what you've written.

Of course, that's not all a good editor will do. As a dispassionate reader (as well as an experienced one) a good editor will be able to see your book through the eyes of the market: they'll understand what works and what doesn't, and will be able to advise you accordingly. This isn't something many writers can achieve by themselves.

But who said anything about doing it by yourself? You'll have friends and acquaintances you can call on – so call on them. Choose carefully though; you don't want a negative opinion to spoil a good relationship. But you should be able to think of someone not too close (but close enough) to read what you've written and give you an honest opinion. If they're willing, make it clear what you want from them. You need someone to give it to you straight: does it work? are there any problems? what improvements can you make?

Exercise 7.3

Think about this now. Who could you call on to give you an honest – and accurate – opinion of your work? Cast the net far and wide and be prepared to consider people who might not otherwise be among your intimate circle – they could be the most useful!

The devil is in the detail

Style is subjective, and what one reader – or editor – admires can be anathema to another. There's no accounting for taste. What you can do, however, is make your prose as accurate as possible. There are several good books on the market without resorting to Lynne Truss's pedantic (but entertaining) *Eats, Shoots and Leaves*. The truth is, the English language is dynamic, evolving all the time – whether we like it or not – in the light of trends (such as text-speak) and the influence of other languages. (Our vocabulary is generally thought to be at least half a million words strong, compared to, say, French which has only a tenth of that.) Shakespeare alone was responsible for minting at least 2000 neologisms (new words) many of which were, undoubtedly, dialect words which he simply brought to a wider audience.

So we needn't be too precious about the language. There are, however, certain basic standards a writer ought to strive to meet. And here are a few of the most common mistakes to keep as a check-list. If you can't be your own editor, at least be your own sub:

'Learn to be your own harshest critic, but never be afraid to recognise your strengths and promote them/fight for them.'

Gary William Murning, novelist

'Style is subjective, and what one reader – or editor – admires can be anathema to another. There's no accounting for taste. What you can do, however, is make your prose as accurate as possible.'

Accommodate

Achievable

Acquired

Aggravate

Appropriately

Benefitted

Biased or biassed (both are correct)

Bored *with* (not of)

Bare all/one's soul (not bear)

Business

Commendable

Committed

Conscientious

Creditable

Debatable

Definite

Desperate

Diligence

Diligent

Eliminate

Equalise (Equalize in the US)

Exaggerate

Focused, focussed (either is acceptable)

Forty

Four

Fulfil

Fulfilled

Fulfilling

Fulfilment

Hear, hear (not here, here)

Humorous

Humour

Immediately

Independent

Industriously

Ineligible

Intelligent

Intelligible

(un)necessarily

(un)necessary

Occasional

Occasionally

Occur

Occurred

Occurrence

Occurring

Perceive

Perception

Perceptive

Practice (noun) 'He needs practice; with practice she will . . . '

Practise (verb) 'He needs to practise; she must practise . . . '

Resourceful

Separate

Thorough

And beware the spell check. How many disciples did Jesus have? None, but he did have twelve fully committed and specially chosen decibels.

And as for the apostrophe . . .

We all do it. I've probably done it somewhere in this book and the eagle-eyed amongst you will have spotted it. That darned 'comma in the air' can be a real menace; most of us know (even if we make mistakes while typing quickly) the difference between you're (*you are*) and your (as in, *belonging to you*). It's (*it is*) the possessive apostrophe that really creates problems. And if it does so for you, it might help to know that it's (*it is* . . . that's – *that is* – one exception to the following rule) a relic of an archaic way of speaking.

Several hundred years ago, the possessive was rendered (largely) with an extra 'e'. So, the swill belonging to the pigs would be 'pigges swill' and the apostrophe (') simply became a shorthand way to replace the 'e' when it was dropped. Thus the 'groceres apostrophe' is now the 'grocer's apostrophe' and the (') replaces the missing letter just as it does when you say 'it's – *it is* – a fine day'. One notable exception that always catches people out (including me) is the possessive 'its'. You'd think – given what I've just said – that if you want to say something belongs to the object 'it' you'd add an apostrophe. But you don't. 'It's' only ever means 'it is', not 'the thing belonging to it'. Don't you just love the English language?

Summing Up

- Take the greatest care with what you do, and check it when you can. Put it away, and get others whose opinion you can trust, to read what you've written before showing it to anyone in the industry.

- Avoid the common pitfalls. A simple grammar (-ar, not –er!) can help, but – as ever – practice (-ice, ice baby!) makes perfect.

- The English language isn't precious; we don't have an Academy to protect it (unlike the French) but it pays to stick to certain rules. In particular, you aren't ever 'bored of' something (like this book) – you are bored with it.

Chapter Eight

Short Story Writing

In this chapter you'll be introduced to some of the basic elements of one of the most popular – and most difficult – fictional forms: the short-story.

- *How 'long' is 'short'?*

- *Do short stories have a specific word limit?*

- *What are the key ingredients of a great short story?*

Short story writing is a little bit like writing poetry. Both demand the same kind of detail and focus; both could be regarded as a distillation of something larger, something which in other circumstances might be longer – like a novel. So – apart from the fact that it's shorter than a novel and doesn't rhyme or scan like poetry – what exactly is a short story?

Here's one I made earlier

That's actually a rather difficult question to answer. A short story can be so many different things, from Ernest Hemingway's famous six-worder ('For sale: baby shoes, never worn') to something approaching the length of a small novella. So in the best 'Blue Peter' traditions, to help answer this question – here's one I made earlier. It's in three parts (they don't have to be); it could almost be a chapter from a longer piece of fiction (but it isn't). What it is, is a short story. But why?

Exercise 8.1

Read 'Cybermummy' now and, as you do, ask yourself this question: what (apart from its length) do you think marks this piece of writing as a short story.

'Cybermummy'

1

'So, world – here I am!'

No, don't be so silly; I can't possibly start like that. I can't possibly begin my first ever blog-post in such a corny, unimaginative and downright silly way. Ok then, so how *do* I begin? What can I say that will get people reading? How do I make myself stand out from the blogging crowd? Hmmm. Not as easy as you think, this blogging lark.

I know; I've got it! I'll start by writing something funny. Yes – I'll tell a funny story. Ok, then. Funny. Here we go.

Monday 3rd July – Supermarket Sweep

You know how it is, you're in the supermarket and you're steering the trolley carefully, narrowly avoiding all the grannies chatting to each other right across the aisle; you steer a precise course down the centre, equidistant from each shelf, because if you didn't your little one would be stretching out his arms and reaching out for all those tempting-looking jars and cans. And you'll be half-way down the aisle before you realise the shelves are being emptied and that trail of devastation – those smashing bottles and those tins of baked-beans bouncing – is all your doing. Well, not strictly speaking yours – his: that cute, blue-eyed, blond-haired little cherub who is even now beaming like the very sun at all the people running round with mops and brushes and melting the hearts of all the pensioners tut-tutting at his mum. You know what I'm talking about, don't you? No? Well in that case this is probably not the blog for you.

Is it just me, or do all parents go through such public traumas when they try to go about their daily business? I need to know; that's why I'm sharing this with you. If you're a mum like me and you're as harassed as I am, let's commiserate. If you're not, if you're a super-mum and things like this don't happen, then I want to know your secret.

And if you're not a mum at all, go find yourself another blog to read (lol)! Back soon!

Yes, that's perfect. I like that, I like that lots. It sets up just the right light-hearted tone whilst at the same time making it absolutely clear what I'm about and why I'm here – my new cyberspace home! Of course, they don't know the real reason do they? Why should they? Let's just leave it there for now, shall we? Hit 'Publish Post' and see what happens. Ok then? Here goes!

Success! Your post has now been published. If you want to read it, click <u>here</u>.

I suppose I'd better have a look at it, just to make sure.

2

Oh – my – God. I mean, oh – my – f**king – God. Just look at the number of comments she gets! Forty five! Forty-fucking-five for that wet fart of a blog-post. I don't believe you morons, really I don't. I mean – look! Look at Supermarket Sweep – quality writing; entertaining; educating. And what does it get? Three comments and a bit of Swedish porn-spam. My God in Heaven, where's the justice?

Of course, they all feel sorry for her don't they? 'Course they do. I mean, just look at some of the drivel they've written; look at the bleedin' comments section:

Here's (((((Hugs)))))) honey, hoping you'll feel better soon.

You said that yesterday, luvvie, and at roughly the same time . . .

Aw, poor you! You must be really suffering xxxxx

Xxxx? Spider kisses.

What's up kid? Sending you some positive Twitter vibes . . .

What's up kid? What's up? She's made that abundantly clear, you arse-hole – she's a self-centred, hypochondriacal attention-seeking and manipulating BITCH – 'sweetie'! Well, at least you got the 'kid' bit right – she is; and a bloody big one too.

Oh, stop bitching Gina. It'll do no good. And anyway, there's a pile of washing that you should be doing. Chances are at this rate it'll still be here when he gets home from work.

And of course, he doesn't understand what I'm doing blogging, does he? No. He'll come back home from work and take one look at the overflowing washing basket, sigh a bit and ask me: 'busy day, love?'

Then he'll start to load the washer, probably telling me to go and put my feet up, have a cup of tea, relax. Then after he's bathed Benjy, read him a story and put him to bed he'll probably offer to make supper. Oh God, why can't he just shout at me? Why doesn't he call me a lazy good-for-nothing, sponging off him, doing nothing all day but a bit of silly blogging? It's what I am, after all. And what I do. Why doesn't he hate me? God, I'd have some fabulous posts to write if he did.

3

'Hi honey . . . '

'I'm in here, on the sofa.'

'Hi gorgeous.' I offer him my cheek. 'Where's Benjamin?'

'Still napping. He's been upstairs for the last hour and-a-half.'

'And you've been blogging, I see. Let me have a look.' He takes the lap-top and sits down.

'This is good,' he says. 'I like this one.' But I'm not listening.

'I think I'll give up blogging,' I'm saying to him. 'No, really. I'm through with it.'

'Really?' He sounds surprised.

'Really. I mean, what's it for? No-one ever reads this stuff.'

'I read it.'

'You don't count. I mean none of the others read it.'

'Others?' Oh my God I'm married to a parrot.

'The mummy-bloggers,' I explain. It's like dealing with a child. 'The inner circle, the big cheese bloggers with their groups and conferences and PR pitches.'

'Ah the cyber mummies,' he says.

And I have to laugh. Even though I want to cry.

'Don't you sometimes get that feeling, just occasionally, every now and then?'

'Not often,' he says. But I can tell that he's not listening.

'Don't you sometimes want to throw the whole thing out, chuck it in, give it up completely and go into the country and just, I don't know, hug a tree or something? I do. Sometimes I really don't know where the next blog post's coming from; sometimes I really don't think I can match the quality blogs I'm reading; sometimes I just don't want to be a blogger any more.'

'Uh-huh? Then what happens?'

'Oh, I don't know; I get an idea; something happens. Or I get an email; someone offering me something.'

'Ah . . . '

'Yes, ah . . . '

'And you realise it's actually quite lucrative.'

Oh God, he heard me.

'I suppose it is, yes. I do.'

'And so you sit down at your lap-top and you tap-tap-tap away, and before you know it, you've got another post written and the comments start to come in and the whole cycle starts all over again.'

'Put like that, I suppose it does,' I tell him.

'Of course it does. But it doesn't have to. It's really got to you, this blogging lark, hasn't it? You're an addict. You can't live without it.'

'No I'm not. I could give it up right now . . . '

'But you can't. Or you won't. It amounts to the same thing.'

'It doesn't.'

'What it boils down to is you keep thinking about chucking it all in but you never do. And never will.'

I say nothing; never do. Instead, I turn my back on him and get the lap-top out. After all, there are comments to be written on the posts that I've been reading. That's the way I'm going. If they won't come to me, I'll go to them, join in. I'll comment on everything they're saying until curiosity gets the better of them all and they come looking for me, commenting on my posts. Now, where was I? Ah yes, this post:

They don't realise how hard it is for me. I feel so tired all the time. It's so depressing and I feel like I'm missing out on all the fun that Kylie and her mum should both be having.

Now if I just scroll down to the final comment. Yes, there it is again. I've found it:

What's up kid? Sending you some positive Twitter vibes . . .

Do you want to add a comment? Silly question. Of course I do. So click 'Add Comment'. Here we go.

Aw, hun, it must be awful for you. Here's sending you some cyber-love. I'm thinking of you. Love, Online Mum of One

Hit 'Send'.

From the top

Ok, so it's short. I said it would be. But what else makes what you've just read a short story? Let's take it apart, starting with the title.

Because you're working on such a small scale in a short story, the title is an integral part of what you're writing. It should immediately link to the story as well as giving the reader something to think about. 'Cybermummy' raises a number of questions (what are we dealing with here – a robot?) as well as setting the scene (in this case 'online') for the story.

Next, perspective. The story is told from the point of view of just one character, Gina. It attempts to get under her skin, to see the world through her eyes and to inhabit her mind to an extent that would be uncomfortable or repetitive in a longer work of fiction. Don't get me wrong; this kind of thing is done in longer fiction. There are plenty of first person novels, a good many of which give the reader an intimate knowledge of the narrator's psyche. But novels can (and often do) do a lot more besides, such as deal with different points of view, have multiple characters and a wider range of settings. Short stories, by and large, don't. Which brings us to the next characteristic – setting.

There is often only one setting in a short story – and in the case of 'Cybermummy' it's really the narrator's head. We don't actually need to know anything about the sofa she's sitting on or the make of the computer that she's using. We don't need to know and – because this is a short story – we haven't room to tell. So only those details that are strictly necessary get to be included. And this goes for any short story setting. So, you've set your story in a field. You can't afford the space to bang on about its acreage, the soil or the type of grass that's growing. Unless, that is, any one of those is vitally important to the story. So, if it's about a horse, the grass might be vitally important. But the clouds scudding across a windswept sky won't be. Remember – only the details that count!

Exercise 8.2

Think about this definition for a moment. What 'hints' or clues are we given about Gina's character in the story 'Cybermummy'? What other elements in this piece give you an idea of what sort of person she is and what motivates her?

Less is more

In the final section of the story, we're actually introduced via dialogue to Gina's husband. He doesn't get very much to say – in fact this section is only a little over 400 words long – before Gina goes back to her computer. But I bet you could construct a pretty accurate character summary from even this microcosm.

Exercise 8.3

Try this for yourself now. Gina's husband doesn't even have a name – so marginal is he – but in this short exchange between husband and wife I think we probably learn all we need to learn about the man who's married to Gina.

So, what sort of person is he? Make a list of some of the adjectives that you think might apply to this shadow of a character. If you want to take things further, you could even construct an entire CV for the man. What sort of job do you think he's just come home from, for example? Certainly not something like lion-taming!

Pay-off time

Finally, of course, the story has to have some kind of pay-off – an epiphany, conclusion, denouement or 'ah ha' moment or whatever you choose to call it. Pretty obviously, in Cybermummy, the pay-off is when something significant about Gina's character is revealed – both to us as readers and, I suspect, to Gina herself. It's an obvious feature, but one that a surprising number of novice short story writers seem to overlook. Basically, something has got to happen. It can be subtle; it probably isn't going to be earth-shattering. But it needs to be there. Short stories in which world changing events occur probably aren't going to be short stories. The denouement need be nothing more than a brief moment of insight. But it makes the 'story' a story (as opposed to a monologue or case-study).

'Good short stories are rather like suggestions: the writer gives hints, leaves clues; the reader's imagination comes up with the conclusion.'

Now even shorter . . . Flash Fiction

In recent years there's been a trend to make short stories ever shorter. Flash, or 'micro' fiction as it's sometimes called, is now an established sub-genre. But the rules are still the same: you don't explain, you don't wallow, you don't amplify or indulge your taste for purple prose. You point the reader in the right direction and let him or her do all the work.

Here's an example from a creative writing student of mine:

The Decision, by Sandy Calico

Maggie drove home on autopilot, replaying the conversation with her mother.

'I'm not sure Phil and I will be together much longer.'

'Phil's a good man.'

'Mum, he's boring me to death.'

She noticed something on the road ahead and stopped the car. A male pheasant stood crestfallen, looking down at his mate, lying motionless.

Maggie, forlorn, stared with him.

She reached for her mobile.

'Phil, we need to talk.'

Words unspoken

Of course, it's disingenuous of me to suggest that the reader does *all* the work; writing good flash fiction is a lot harder than it appears. It inverts the writer's normal modus operandi and has him or her struggling to avoid writing too much, rather than straining to write anything at all.

In essence, I suppose good short stories are rather like suggestions: the writer gives hints, leaves clues; the reader's imagination comes up with the conclusion. And flash fiction takes this one stage further – not so much painting a picture as merely *suggesting* what might be happening.

'The rules for flash fiction are still the same as for the short story: don't explain, don't wallow, don't amplify or indulge your taste for purple prose. Point the reader in the right direction and let him or her do all the work.'

Summing up

- Title: this really needs to set the story up in some way, as well as grab the reader's attention.
- Perspective: almost inevitably the short story will be from the point of view of just one person. In some cases, he or she will be the only character.
- Setting: keep the surroundings simple because the setting is probably the protagonist's head.
- Denouement: something has to happen, but make sure it's something simple.

'The story has to have some kind of pay-off – an epiphany, conclusion, denouement or "ah ha" moment.'

Chapter Nine

The Play's the Thing

In this chapter you'll be introduced to some of the basic elements of scriptwriting, examining some of the basic principles that apply to all forms of drama and looking in detail at adapting a piece of writing for radio.

The art of the playwright is probably the noblest among the various creative writing genres. The act of putting on plays, performing an author's words on stage and presenting drama before an audience is as old as civilisation itself. You'd think, therefore, that it might be the form most practised by aspiring authors, the one that came most easily to the would-be writer.

But nothing could be further from the truth. Scriptwriting – whether for the stage, television or radio or the cinema – is one of the most specialist and technically most demanding forms of writing – and yet also, probably, one of the most satisfying.

By their words shall ye know them

The late John Mortimer was once asked why, early in his literary career, he'd given up writing novels in favour of plays. He replied – 'you never catch anyone reading your novel on the train. But having an entire roomful of actors speaking your lines is one of the best feelings a writer can have.' A script isn't meant to be read, on the page; it is written to be performed. The words a playwright pens have to be spoken aloud. Furthermore, the underlying emotions, reactions and tensions have to be shown to the audience. That, of course, is the skill of a great actor. But it is the author who provides the words on which they must base their performance.

'Scriptwriting – whether for the stage, television or radio or the cinema – is one of the most specialist and technically most demanding forms of writing – and yet also, probably, one of the most satisfying.'

There is a link between the 'less is more' approach of short story writing (as discussed in the previous chapter) and the art of writing an effective script. Although – to a greater or lesser extent, depending on the medium – stage directions will be included, in plays it is the *words* that carry the drama and a play is always more than merely dialogue.

Exercise 9.1

Look back at 'The Decision' by Sandy Calico (page 65). How would you go about adapting this for the stage? What would need to be added? And what – if anything – would you remove?

Basic ingredients

It should be clear just from thinking about the above exercise that certain essential ingredients need to be added to make a successful play. If actors and directors are to understand what an author intends they're going to need some help. This usually comes in the form of telling them:

- The setting – where does the action take place? If there's more than one setting, the play will need dividing into different scenes.

- Stage directions – what's happening either as the lines are being spoken, or immediately before or afterwards?

- Who's on stage – entrances and exits are obviously vital, and are usually included in the opening stage directions and then supplemented as different characters walk on and off the stage (or in and out of the scene).

- Where they are on the stage. There are a number of shorthand ways of telling an actor where to stand – CS (centre-stage); SL or SR (stage left/ right) and so on.

- How the lines are to be spoken – include some emphasis (e.g. 'whispering') if it's important (and if it isn't obvious from just reading the words). But be careful not to litter your script with too much information. The performers need space to add their own interpretation of what you've written.

Exercise 9.2

Choose a story you've written – or create a new one – and start to assemble a script using the above list as your starting point.

You'll need to consider some of the basic elements of good storytelling we've discussed in previous chapters and in particular know the 'arc' of your story. Then divide the story into scenes either according to the setting or else based on what is happening at a particular time in the narrative. Finally, start writing the dialogue and adding essential directions.

Your script should look something like this:

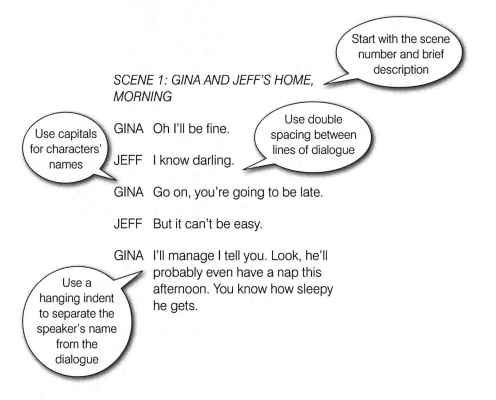

SCENE 1: GINA AND JEFF'S HOME, MORNING

> Start with the scene number and brief description

> Use capitals for characters' names

GINA   Oh I'll be fine.

JEFF   I know darling.

> Use double spacing between lines of dialogue

GINA   Go on, you're going to be late.

JEFF   But it can't be easy.

GINA   I'll manage I tell you. Look, he'll probably even have a nap this afternoon. You know how sleepy he gets.

> Use a hanging indent to separate the speaker's name from the dialogue

Be adaptable . . .

You might recognise this as a very basic adaptation of part of my short story, *Cybermummy*. Although adaptation is by no means an easy option, it may help if you're attempting playwriting for the first time to look back at something you've already written or an idea that you've already formed. Shakespeare, after all, didn't start from scratch but was indebted to a number of authors and their works – to Holinshed's *Chronicles* (1587) for the plots of the English history plays; to Plutarch's *Parallel Lives* for Greek and Roman drama.

Writing for radio

'UK radio has a voracious appetite for drama. As such, it is probably one of the best starting points for an author eager to give scriptwriting a go.'

UK radio has a voracious appetite for drama. As such, it is probably one of the best starting points for an author eager to give scriptwriting a go and because of this I'm going to spend the rest of this chapter discussing this medium in some detail as well as presenting a substantial extract from a radio script of my own so that you can see precisely how to lay your own script out.

Getting to know you

Of course, as with any form of creative writing, getting to know the genre is essential. Fortunately, with radio drama, this is as easy as owning a transistor radio or – these days – a computer. Even a mobile 'phone might do. The point is you need to listen across the entire range of radio drama output, both in order to find out which 'slot' is best for your material and to learn from the work of successful radio dramatists.

Let's deal with the slots, first of all. Although the BBC has cut back on some of its output it is still by far the major player in the field with a daily 45 minute complete drama on Radio Four together with serialisations of classic works in both hour-long slots (afternoons and evenings) and fifteen minute episodes (daily, following *Woman's Hour* and repeated at seven forty five each evening). Then there's Radio Three, broadcasting longer complete plays in evening slots, usually (but not exclusively) on Sunday evenings. There may be opportunities in local radio, too; there are certainly intermittent openings on BBC World Service. And this is to say nothing of independent radio providers.

Where do I start?

Having spent some time listening across the range of output, you'll have a pretty good idea of where in the schedules (and which station) your work is destined. Thankfully, the BBC has made it easy to make contact through a resource called writersroom. Sending your script to the BBC writersroom is almost certainly the best place to start. If they like what they read, they'll hand the project to a producer – either in-house or someone working for one of the many independent production companies commissioned by the BBC to produce radio drama.

Exercise 9.3

Have a look at the BBC writersroom now. You can find it at http://www.bbc.co.uk/writersroom/ and it would be time well spent to browse the resources and advice available whether or not you intend at some point to submit a script.

Just a minute . . .

But before all that, of course, you must complete your script. People say radio drama is effective because the 'pictures' are so good. These, of course, are all in the listeners head and this element of partnership between author and listener certainly has strong resonances with the principles of short story writing which were discussed in the previous chapter. It also makes unique technical demands that you, as author, need to overcome.

Sounding off

The most obvious device for painting a picture in the listener's head is – apart from the word, of course – the sound effect. You can conjure up all manner of scenes with just a few, well-chosen sounds. Your job – as author – is to suggest them and to do so briefly. If you want to set a scene outdoors, in Summer for example, with birds singing and children playing it's not necessary to include precise ornithological instructions or to specify the age of the children and what games they're playing. 'FX' is the commonly-used shorthand

'I think David Hare's advice is best. Basically, be prepared to produce your own plays. Get them up on the boards however, wherever you can. That's what I did with my first play, and that experience led to five years of producing plays for others.'

Sue Guiney, novelist and playwright

for 'sound effects' and you'll notice that – for radio, where such effects are all important – they're both underlined and written in capital letters. Here's how it's usually done:

SCENE 1: GINA AND JEFF'S HOME, MORNING

<u>FADE UP DISTANT SOUND OF BABY CRYING, FOLLOWED BY FRONT DOOR OPENING.</u>

GINA   'Bye darling!

JEFF   'Bye love. See you later . . . Sounds like you're going to have your hands full today.

<u>FX: (LOUDER) BABY CRYING</u>

GINA   Oh I'll be fine.

JEFF   I know darling.

GINA   Go on, you're going to be late.

JEFF   But it can't be easy.

GINA   I'll manage I tell you. Look, he'll probably even have a nap this afternoon. You know how sleepy he gets.

JEFF   If you're sure -

<u>FX: BRIEF KISS</u>

JEFF   - And if he has a nap this afternoon you never know, you might even get some time to put your feet up. (WALKING AWAY) You never know, you might even do a bit of blogging. Bye.

GINA   (TO SELF) Oh, yes of course. Keep in touch with the news world. Citizen journalism and all that. Because, that's where it's at isn't it darling. Blogger, Twitter . . .

<u>FX: DOOR CLOSES. BABY CRYING</u>

GINA   In a minute love, in a minute . . . (TO SELF) Well Jeff darling, you suggested it. Ever the dutiful wife, and all that. 'Love, honour and obey.' Except for the 'obey' bit. Well, and the honour, come to that. And love? (PAUSE) Oh well, there's no time like the present, baby or no baby. (CALLING UPSTAIRS) Oh do stop crying Benjy dear. I'll be up in a minute.

<u>SOUND OF LAP-TOP BEING OPENED, KEYBOARD CLICKS , WINDOWS START-UP CHIME. BABY CRIES FADING</u>

GINA   Now, where were we . . . Let me see. Just need to get this first post finished and then I'll be with you. Oh do stop crying Benjy. Please!

<u>FX: LAP-TOP KEYBOARD – RAPID TAP TAP</u>

'You can conjure up all manner of scenes with just a few, well-chosen sounds. Your job – as author – is to suggest them and to do so briefly.'

Need2Know

Less is more

Of course, sound effects are only one of the things the radio dramatist has to be aware of. Without pictures, televisual and cinematic effects such as a glance into the middle distance (conveying longing, or regret for instance) are unavailable. On screen, a picture – if not worth a thousand words – can certainly replace a couple of hundred.

But beware. This doesn't mean that on radio you've got to fall back on having the characters describe what's happening to each other ('oh look, darling – you've just hit that pedestrian!'). Remember the 'show, not tell' techniques discussed earlier and be creative with your exposition. Apart from the fact that having characters describe what's happening for the benefit of listeners would make for tedious and bloated radio, remember – as with short stories – you're in the business of suggestion. Less really is sometimes more.

The play wot I wrote

All of which leaves only one thing, really. And that's for you to have a go. But before you do you should be aware that adapting a story for a medium like radio involves far more than merely making a script of the original. Scenes that work perfectly well on the page may never transfer successfully to a page or pages of script. And subtleties of narrative that – in prose – can be rendered in just a couple of lines may require the writing of entirely new scenes. In other words, the play will almost always be a work of art in its own right rather than a mere 'version' of the story on which it's based.

Exercise 9.4

Consider this now. Think about a film version of a book you've read. What had to be changed in order to bring the book to the screen? Which scenes are in the book, but not the film? And what had to be left out? Was the adaptation a success, in your opinion?

Summing Up

■ Plays aren't merely stories 'acted out' on stage or in the studio. The technical demands of drama mean that a writer will have to think about telling a story in a different way.

■ A great place to start for the budding dramatist is radio. Listen to as much radio drama as you can to get a feel for the medium.

■ Remember, a play is a unique work of art in its own right and not merely a 'version' of a story that already exists, either in your own head or on the pages of a book.

Chapter Ten

Genre Fiction

In this chapter we'll take a more detailed look at some of the different categories of fiction writing, examining the distinctive characteristics of several of the most popular literary genres and introducing some of the conventions followed by genre writers.

- What are the basic categories of fiction and why do they matter?
- How do the basic principles of good fiction writing integrate with the rules of each genre?
- Is genre writing an easy option?

Rules is rules

Each of the genres we'll be discussing has its own distinct conventions and rules. It isn't enough to pay them lip service. Readers of genre fiction are a fastidious bunch; they know what they like and they like to know what to expect.

As always, if you're considering writing genre fiction you'll have read widely in your chosen field. You'll know that you need to understand the rules and the conventions fully even if you intend at some point to break them. But don't expect to write a fantasy adventure without first understanding what a fantasy adventure is about.

A number of very basic rules apply to each of the main genres, and I'll be discussing these under each of the headings in this chapter. But remember – whatever genre you're writing, the writing itself must be the best you can produce and the story must conform to the basic principles discussed in chapter four. Basically, this means strong characters, natural dialogue, gripping action and a big emotional or physical denouement. These are the essential ingredients of your story-telling. Get them right and you'll probably master any of the following genres.

Exercise 10.1

Before reading on, think about the different 'rules' that apply to the following genres. What do you think is essential to make, say, a 'chick lit' book, well – chick lit? Can you identify the themes and stylistic conventions that each genre relies upon?

- Fantasy.
- Romantic.
- Horror.
- Sci-fi.
- Historical.

'Remember – whatever genre you're writing, the writing itself must be the best you can produce.'

Sub genres

Of course, it's never enough for any field of human endeavour to be merely arranged into half a dozen different categories. Most of the genres mentioned here can be further sub-divided into several smaller areas. A work of crime fiction, for example, might be a police procedural novel, a cosy rural mystery (think *Miss Marple*) or a country house whodunit to name just three. It's probably best not to get too bogged down in the minutiae of classification and just get on with the business of writing. As already stated, what you want to write will probably at least in part be based on the kind of thing you like to read, so the chances are that you'll instinctively know which genre best suits your ambitions.

Exercise 10.2

Consider this for a moment. What are your own tastes in fiction? Which genre is your favourite? And if you're thinking of adding to the canon, do you plan to follow the formula or try and 'break the mould'?

Fantasy

In a sense, of course, all fiction is 'fantasy' of one sort or another. But as a genre, fantasy is about the creation of magical worlds and the doing of amazing things. The whole point of it is that the 'normal' isn't and the impossible can happen – and not in a 'mere' superhuman sense. Fantasy isn't about creating stories where people succeed against impossible odds using normal means. The whole idea is that normal rules no longer apply. People, in other words, can fly; animals can talk; spells are cast; unimagined worlds exist beneath our feet or in the space between quantum particles in our heads.

If all of that makes it seem like the stuff of children's fairy stories, think again. If writing convincingly about the real world is difficult enough, how much harder is it going to be to create and then write about a world that doesn't exist? It has to be believable, yet incredible; magical, yet real; supernatural, yet normal. Because – however extraordinary – the fantasy world your characters inhabit is, after all, *their* reality. Your job as a writer is to make that appear perfectly normal for the reader. And this means all the usual expectations of good fiction writing apply just as much to fantasy, if not more.

Romantic fiction

Although everyone's heard of Mills and Boon (one of the most successful publishing enterprises in any genre) the reputation of Romantic Fiction isn't always as strong as it deserves to be. No doubt there once was time when slightly timid, subordinate secretaries fell into the strong, masterful arms of tyrant bosses who had previously been guilty of making their lives something of a misery (not too far removed from Jane Eyre and Mr Rochester?) but the modern reader of romantic fiction is a lot more demanding. This means – more often than not – that the psychological flaws and motivations of characters will be overtly explored, even though the characters still frequently conform to one or more of the broad stereotypes. But these stereotypes aren't necessarily the stereotypes drawn from real-life romance.

Understanding and appreciating the escapist element of romantic fiction is crucial to writing it with any degree of success. Most of us will meet and marry people from a narrowly-defined social (and even geographical) area – princes don't often marry paupers. But in romantic fiction, readers are trained to expect the unexpected. And these expectations are buried deep in literature. 'Reader, I married him,' says Jane Eyre; Elizabeth Bennett overcomes her prejudice and Darcy his pride on their journey to the aisle. It is often the overcoming of otherwise insurmountable odds – love in spite of circumstance – that makes for the most satisfying romantic fiction.

Chick lit

The sub-genre 'chick lit' tends to deal less in these 'fairytale' scenarios and instead takes a more down-to-earth approach. The conflict is likely to be domestic, rather than social and deals more with the kind of everyday obstacles (divorce, step-children, money and embarrassing ex's) that are often placed in the path of true love. But in both cases readers will expect to have their pulses quickened by some jolly good descriptive writing. For the romantic novelist of either hue, the challenge lies in making an unlikely marriage (or relationship – let's not be too old-fashioned) ultimately seem the most natural – and unstoppable – thing in the world.

Lad lit

Whereas chick lit is most certainly a sub-genre of romantic fiction, Lad Lit is in many ways a category all its own. In most people's opinion, it can't be said to be an offshoot of anything else at all really.

Whatever its antecedents, Lad Lit emerged from nowhere as quite a recent phenomenon through the works of authors like Nick Hornby and Tony Parsons. In many ways it might be thought of as a simple branch of general, popular fiction – but with the thematic unity of having a young, male protagonist with a sometimes slightly chauvinistic or hapless outlook. But these strikingly similar thematic tendencies give it slightly more than many would like to admit in common with good old romantic fiction and chick lit. It might be stretching a point to say that Lad Lit should be regarded as a sub-genre to this overarching category, but the similarity (in all but the sex of the main protagonist) is inescapable.

'The characteristics of writing for children and teens are the same as in any form of fiction – strong plot, engaging characters and plenty of conflict.'

Tamsyn Murray, author of *My So-Called Afterlife*

Our hero often has to overcome obstacles placed before him by his own defects of personality, and the denouement usually involves a lesson learnt, a new phase embarked upon and – not infrequently – the concluding influence of a good woman.

Writing for children and young adults

The biggest mistake any writer can make is to think that writing for children and young adults is somehow easier than writing for anyone else. If anything, it's harder. There are all kinds of linguistic and thematic issues to address, to say nothing of the fact that – in many ways – the younger the audience, the less forgiving. In the words of one well-known children's author, 'you can't get away with anything'. Not that you'd want to, of course.

Writing for children, together with YA fiction, covers almost the entire genre range of adult books with subjects ranging from the fantasy novels of Harry Potter to the earthy reality of a character like Jacqueline Wilson's *Tracy Beaker*. In writing for a younger audience, authors are often required to be more overtly aware of the 'moral' of the story they are telling. There is usually a requirement that certain basic standards of behaviour are – if not maintained – at least ultimately rewarded. But apart from that, write as you would for an adult readership – know your target audience and keep them turning pages!

Illustrated children's books

Writing illustrated books for small children is usually something undertaken as a partnership between author and illustrator, unless you happen to do both. As an author, if you've got an idea for an entertaining story based on vivid, engaging characters (be they animal, vegetable or mineral!) the next step (apart from writing the words, of course) is usually to approach a potential publisher who will then – if they like the idea – put you in touch with an illustrator.

'I'd advise anyone who wants to write YA to make sure they speak to actual teenagers and to use that experience in their writing. Oh, and avoid slang; there's nothing more cringe-making to teens than an out-of-date in-phrase.

Tamsyn Murray, author of *My So-Called Afterlife*

Horror

Horror has a long and distinguished literary history dating back even further than one of its best known progenitors, Mary Shelley's *Frankenstein*. The genre covers a wide range of subjects and styles but what all have in common is the desire to stimulate the same emotional response in the reader – fear. Whether that's done through a traditional M.R. James ghost story or something altogether less subtle by the likes of (for example) Stephen King doesn't really matter. Horror usually involves a good dollop of the supernatural and is designed to get the reader's pulse racing, as well as make them a little more cautious about locking the doors when they retire for the night.

Sci fi

From *War of the Worlds* to *Star Trek* to *The Hitchhikers Guide to the Galaxy*, science fiction covers a vast array of narrative styles. What they all have in common is that they take scientific fact and make something fantastical – but plausible – from it. The secret of good Sci Fi is knowing the science, and there can be no short cut. Readers of science fiction know their stuff and will be hot on your heels if you don't know yours.

Historical fiction

The historical novel is something of a specialist area; it can be anything from popular 'action' writing such as the *Sharpe* series of novels by Bernard Cornwell (set at the time of the Napoleonic Wars) to something altogether more serious, like the 2011 Booker-nominated *Jamrach's Menagerie* by Carol Birch.

What is usually common to all historical fiction is its starting point: historical fact. This kind of writing almost always – no, *always* – begins with a real historical incident or event and adds imagination to the mix. No history, however recent, is ever complete. Adding an author's imagination to the business of assembling a historical jigsaw can lead to some immensely satisfying results and, occasionally, not a little genuine historical insight.

But therein lies the rub. If your novel is based in Roman Britain you'll have to become – if you're not already – a Roman historian. Because historical fiction fills the gaps between what we know and what we imagine, the facts have to be rock-solid. It's no use guessing. If you don't know, you must find out. The fun of that, of course, is that in finding out you'll probably discover that no two academic historians agree on what actually happened anyway – which might provide you with useful inspiration for your next big plot twist!

Crime and mystery

Crime writing is an enormously popular genre. The standard of writing is high – often competing with so-called 'literary' fiction for serious attention – and it's certainly not to be approached by the faint-hearted. But then, who could possibly be faint-hearted about writing crime fiction? There's no room for the squeamish what with murder, rape, kidnap, torture and any number of other heinous acts to write about.

Within the broad spectrum of crime fiction there exists a panoply of different types of fiction from the tried and trusted 'police procedural' to complex psychological whodunits. Along the way you might find a gifted amateur of the Sherlock Holmes variety, or a little old lady whose strength (apart from a forensic intellect) seems to be that no-one could possibly suspect she could have any interest in – still less, be of any help solving – the crime. But what each of these variants has in common is this: a crime is committed, usually at the beginning or at least, fairly early on, and the remainder of the story consists of unmasking the culprit. We might suspect who it is; we might be mistaken; we might be as confused as the detective whose story we are reading. But there's the key to successful crime writing: the reader is working – struggling – at every stage of the investigation along with the protagonist. We're on his or her side. We're trying to work out whodunit just as they are. We might get there before they do. Or they might pull the criminological equivalent of a rabbit out of a hat in the final pages. Either way, the reader and writer are a team.

Of course teamwork isn't always successful, and some crime novelists have been known to deceive the reader into thinking the butler did it when, in fact, it was the gamekeeper. Although Agatha Christie was quite fond of dishing up the odd red-herring, you have to remember to deceive your main character too. If all along they know precisely what is happening, there'll hardly be a story left to tell.

Erotic fiction

Of all the so-called genres in this chapter, erotic fiction is one of the hardest to analyse. Its aim is all too clear: to excite, to stimulate, to arouse – so far, so good. But precisely *how* erotic fiction goes about its task is more difficult to pin down. Just as human sexuality covers a mind-boggling range of activities, so erotic fiction can cover an extraordinary number of different bedroom scenarios. To say nothing of those occurring anywhere but the bedroom! What is common to them all is this – tension, sexual tension to be precise. The best erotic writing is a tease and just as partial clothing can be more arousing than total nudity, good sex writing will hint and suggest as much as it describes.

But beware. The Bad Sex in Fiction Award awaits anyone whose suggestiveness or hinting becomes too clichéd. The tightrope walked by the writer of erotic fiction is between being too explicit (and thus destroying the sexual tension) and being too coy. There is a whole list of adjectives to avoid at all costs, and finding the right simile or metaphor will take time and patience. The only sure-fire way to succeed is to remember (as stated earlier) to do it your way. Of course, you'll have read all the books and done your research. But be true to the experience you're describing; see it through your eyes and bring to it your own unique understanding and insight.

Summing Up

- The division of fiction into different genres is more than merely an attempt to organise books that share similar subject-matter on the library shelves.

- Genres are an important way of addressing the rules – stylistic and thematic – that different branches of fiction share.

- Whatever the genre, remember the basics still apply. You've got to write a good story with strong characters and a well-crafted plot.

Chapter Eleven

Writing Non-Fiction

In this chapter we'll explore some of the demands of non-fiction writing as well as thinking about its usefulness for the fiction writer.

There are those who consider non-fiction something of a poor relation, hardly worthy of the name 'creative writing'. Needless to say, I'm not one of them. Although there are writers who specialise in either one of the traditional 'creative' pursuits such as writing novels and others who never ever write a word of fiction, a great many authors write both fiction and non-fiction and it is worth considering some of the fundamentals of this specialist area.

Blurring the distinctions

Is biography creative writing? Most people would be happy to accord it such status even though – by definition – it is strictly speaking non-fiction. A biographer wants to unearth the facts about his subject, to present the truth however much it might otherwise be obscured or suppressed.

But is that all? Many biographers are also keen to proffer their opinions, whether overtly or covertly. And, of course, any act of putting pen to paper involves making value judgements – what to retain, what to leave out, where to look, who to ask and so on. At almost every level such editorial decisions could be said – in the broadest sense of the word – to be 'creative'. And – as we've already seen – the line between fact and fiction isn't always easy to define.

'Describing real people in a way that grabs a reader's attention; forming rounded characters capable of driving a story and, indeed, creating a narrative that compels the reader's attention are all essential ingredients of good life writing.'

Types of non-fiction

As we've already seen, there is a wide variety of different types of fiction, to say nothing of completely different writing disciplines such as poetry or drama. It's the same with non-fiction, which can range from autobiography and biography to self-help books like this one, through to academic texts based on a lifetime's research. They may be written out of an author's burning passion for a subject, professional expertise or sometimes simply because an opportunity presents.

Historian and author Guy de la Bédoyère, for example, began an entire series of books about the diarist John Evelyn after a chance encounter with a man who had spent a lifetime amassing a huge archive on the subject, having been born near Evelyn's home in Deptford. A couple of weeks after the meeting the man died unexpectedly, and de la Bédoyère was bequeathed his entire library. As he says, 'those books instantly formed the core of my research and the work dominated the next three to five years of my life.'

'I ended up writing a book on archaeology when I proposed the title and was told that someone else had been commissioned to write it but had failed to deliver. 'Give it to me and you'll have it three months' I told them. It was a risk but they took it and I delivered.'

Guy de la Bédoyère, author and historian

Exercise 11.1

Pursuing non-fiction projects may not be your top priority, but it's worth considering what – if anything – you could write if you had to. That hobby you've spent half a lifetime pursuing – is there a book in it? Or your career – could you make those workplace anecdotes into entertaining reading? Like all writing, non-fiction is a craft and learning it can be of enormous benefit whatever type of writing you intend to specialise in.

Memories are made of this . . .

Life writing – writing about your own or other people's lives – otherwise known as autobiography and biography is a huge market. In recent years the so-called 'misery' memoir of an unhappy childhood has been a surprisingly big literary hit. And writing about your own life takes an author right back to the first maxim of successful prose: to write what you know.

Writing 'what you know' – in the sense of your own life, experiences, relationships and so on – can also be excellent training for fiction writing. Describing real people in a way that grabs a reader's attention; forming rounded characters capable of driving a story and, indeed, creating a narrative that compels the reader to read on are all essential ingredients of good life writing.

This last challenge – to shape the narrative so that it creates an engaging story – is, perhaps, one of the most difficult. Whereas in a work of fiction we can plan and plot, with real life we take what's given – and this might not, ordinarily, make for an entertaining story. We can edit out the boring bits without much difficulty. But creating the momentum that carries a reader through the beginning, middle and end of a life-story requires great care if the result isn't to be a disconnected series of anecdotes.

Of course, for some authors a 'disconnected series of anecdotes' can make both for best-selling and highly entertaining reading. James Herriot's stories of life as a rural vet spring immediately to mind (as do the books of Gervaise Phinn). But even here – however sketchy – there is the outline of a story as the reader follows the eponymous veterinary surgeon from his interview for a position, through marriage and children and – ultimately – retirement: a 'life story' is ever there was one.

Exercise 11.2

Reflect on your own life for a moment. If you were to sit down and write your autobiography, what would the 'story' be? What are the challenges you have faced? And how have they been overcome?

Have notebook, will travel

Throughout the nineteen-eighties and nineties there seemed to be an almost insatiable appetite for good travel writing, with the likes of Bill Bryson, Paul Theroux and Tony Hawks dominating best-seller lists across the English-speaking world. Although the market is not quite as buoyant as it once was, there is still plenty of room on the shelves for original, slightly quirky travel memoirs – to say nothing of the need for good, accurate travel guides.

'The formula for travel writing seems to have boiled down to something like this: an innocent abroad, slightly naïve and possibly other-wordly, gets into all manner of scrapes and ends up with a host of funny stories to be told both against himself and (possibly) against those whom he has visited.'

The formula for travel writing seems to have boiled down to something like this: an innocent abroad, slightly naïve and possibly other-wordly, gets into all manner of scrapes and ends up with a host of funny stories to be told both against himself and (possibly) against those whom he has visited.

The reality, of course, is anything but and the travel writer is nothing if not well-prepared. But all journeys contain an element of the unexpected, and travel writers have to be alert to this as well as be able to notice the things that other people overlook.

The late Robert Robinson may have been best-known for his role as a TV and Radio quizmaster, but he was also an excellent travel writer. In the first of a series of broadcasts from India he travelled from Calcutta to the ancient hill station of Simla and observed that the chief characteristic of the journey wasn't the noise or the language or the heat or the food or anything else that would dominate many another traveller's outlook – but the way people looked at each other 'without challenge'. 'In India,' he wrote, 'everybody stares. But it's not a stare that tries to catch you out'.

Observations like that immediately bring a subject to life in a way that any amount of circumstantial detail ('we caught the crowded train from Calcutta') can't. The good travel writer has an eye – or perhaps that should be, ear – for such telling detail and this is what brings the prose alive.

'The good travel writer has an eye – or perhaps that should be, ear – for telling detail and this is what brings the prose alive.'

Exercise 11.3

You can try this for yourself, writing about any holiday or journey you have undertaken. Surprisingly, the best results sometimes come not from writing about the most spectacular destination you've been to, but from some original observation about a relatively mundane location. Practise distilling the essence of the journey – your experience of it, that is – in as few words as possible, and make each one of them count.

Ghost-writing

No, not penning books about the spirit-world, but providing the words for someone else, usually someone famous without either the time or, perhaps, the skill to write a book for themselves. That's not meant to be cynical. It isn't open to everyone to write books, just as it isn't open to everyone to be a Premiership footballer. But readers will always, it seems, want to read the footballer's story. And a ghost-writer can be an essential collaborator in the process of transforming a series of conversations and interviews into an engaging book.

There is some snobbery about ghost-writers, which is unnecessary to say the least. The skills practised by a good ghost-writer are exactly the same as those used by any author – using words to bring alive a person on the page, shaping events into a satisfying story, addressing conflict and providing resolution.

Textbooks

There's a steady market for textbooks of all shapes and sizes, including those for schools and colleges. Quite a number of these are written by teachers, using their experience of working in classrooms and knowledge both of the subject area and the language levels of the target audience. Although it can be quite a difficult market to break into, if there's a subject you're passionate about and you're prepared to research both the National Curriculum and the existing competition, then by all means approach an educational publisher with an idea. You will need to work out a fairly detailed proposal – probably including a chapter-by-chapter synopsis – and know precisely who the book is for. After that, it will have to fit in with the publisher's planned curriculum coverage. If it does, well done; but if it doesn't you might find – if they like your initial idea – that they start to talk to you about adapting your material to fit their current catalogue.

Summing Up

▪ Although some people consider non-fiction something of a poor relation, even the dedicated fiction-writer can learn something from the unique demands of this form of writing.

▪ With life writing, biography and travel writing the challenge is the same: to shape the narrative into an engaging story and create the momentum that keeps the reader reading.

▪ Like all writing, non-fiction is a craft and learning it can be of enormous benefit whatever type of writing you intend to specialise in.

Chapter Twelve

Towards Publication

In this final chapter we'll look at the world of publishing in general, as well as some of the often-overlooked features associated with successful book sales, such as promotion and publicity.

Publication is the Holy Grail for many writers. They might tell you it's their 'passion for words' and the 'need to write' that keeps them going. But what they really want is publication, which is entirely understandable. After all, what's the point of writing if nobody's reading? (Well, of course, there *is* a point and there are writers happy to do it for its own sake, but that's another story.) But what does 'being published' actually mean? If you're a blogger, every time you write a post you hit the 'publish' button and your words are flung into cyberspace for all to see. And anyone can publish themselves these days on Lulu, a service we'll examine in a bit more detail later. Getting published isn't only difficult to achieve, it's difficult to define.

> 'Getting published or produced is harder than writing the damn stuff in the first place, to be honest.'
>
> Sue Guiney, novelist and playwright

Exercise 12.1

What's your personal writing goal? In an ideal world, would your book be on the 'three-for-two' tables at the front of Waterstone's, or are you simply aiming for a spot on the shelves? Perhaps magazines and periodicals are your targets for publication: if so, which titles do you aspire to and why? Or maybe you're looking to the future with online publishing and e-books: what would make you feel you'd 'made it'?

Publication

Getting published is both harder and easier than ever. The major publishing houses only rarely take on new talent, and the odds against getting an unsolicited manuscript to print are astronomical. But it does happen. Don't be daunted, and – most important of all – believe in your own work. After all, if you don't, it's going to be harder to persuade someone else to.

There are alternatives – down to the printing of a single copy at so-called 'Espresso' machines – to traditional publishing. Small presses still thrive in a niche market, and the Internet means that tiny publishers can have the same shop-window as the big boys (and girls) these days, with very little extra effort.

Then, of course, there's the future: eBooks. There seems little doubt that electronic publishing is not only here to stay, but it's going to keep on growing. Of course, there'll still be books and bookshops, but you've only got to look at the collapse of Borders earlier this year to realise that the old-fashioned way of doing things is becoming unsustainable. With smartphones, the iPad and a host of dedicated eBook readers, downloading a book is becoming as common as downloading an album track. And look what iTunes has done for CD sales!

I think it's an exciting time to be an author. If you're prepared to look at alternative routes to publication, to embrace new technology and give up that dream of retiring on the royalties of your magnum opus, there's never been a better time to get your work before the eyes of readers. And there's nothing like getting an email, out-of-the-blue, from someone, somewhere far away, who has read and enjoyed what you've written.

Isn't that what we're all in it for? Connecting with readers, communicating, sharing thoughts, ideas, and philosophies? As I started by saying way back at the beginning of this book, we've all got something to say. Saying it in the most effective and entertaining way takes practice: and the practice – the writing, day-to-day, the revising, the editing, the polishing – is what the majority of writers enjoy doing most. After all, if they didn't, they wouldn't be writers. Would they?

'It's been hard work to fit everything in around a day job but there's nothing quite like the thrill of holding your own book in your hands and knowing you created it from nothing but an idea and a determination to see the story through.'
Tamsyn Murray, author of *My So-Called Afterlife*

Dear Sir or Madam

I suppose anything that gets your work 'out there' where it can be seen, discussed, enjoyed and – perhaps – paid for counts as being published. Traditionally, though, publication has meant – for books – someone else (the publisher) taking up your work and taking a financial risk by having it type-set, printed, bound and distributed. You, the author, then receive a fraction of the cover price of each book sold in royalties. So it's in your interests both to choose a publisher capable of the widest distribution and to get involved with the promotion of your own book. If only it was all that simple.

In reality, if you're writing fiction, you'll have to have completed your novel, edited it to within an inch of its life and ironed out every single typo, erased each grammatical infelicity, and written a synopsis before you even think about approaching someone with a view to publication. For non-fiction, things are a little different and – in general – you'll be expected to provide a detailed, chapter-by-chapter outline of the book together with a market analysis (who's going to buy it when it's finished?) and at least one sample chapter. On the basis of this outline, a publisher may invite you – with or without obligation – to submit the whole thing at a later date (i.e. when it's written).

Magazines and periodicals often work in a similar way: an editor will want to hear your ideas first (and be persuaded not only that the article is worth writing, but that you're the person to write it).

All this can be quite daunting, and the odds against getting a new work of fiction by an unknown author even read by a major publisher are tiny. Be prepared to wallpaper your sitting room with your rejection letters – if you get any! Some publishers are too 'busy' even for that courtesy. And be prepared to wait . . . and wait . . . and wait. It can take an inordinate amount of time even to get a response. No wonder some authors get impatient.

> 'Agents are a total waste of time. They are only interested in big earners.'
> Guy de la Bédoyère, author and historian

Exercise 12.2

Publishing is changing. Technological advances mean books can be economically produced in units as small as a single copy! There can be a lot to take in, but it's worth knowing a little about the industry you hope to be involved in. How much, for instance, do you know about each of the following?

- Print-runs.
- Slush pile.
- Distribution.
- Type-setting.
- Print-on-demand.
- Proof-reading.
- ISBN.
- Vanity publishing.
- Copyright.

Go your own way

Just as blogging democratises on-line publishing, technology now means that if you're fed up waiting, you could – if you go into it with your eyes wide open – guarantee seeing your book in print, and a lot quicker than if you approach a traditional publisher. Lulu.com is perhaps the best-known self-publishing service, with Amazon's *Createspace* its biggest competitor. Print-on-demand technology (as used by both Lulu.com and *Createspace* but also by an increasing number of mainstream publishers) means that a publisher no longer has to take a financial risk printing lots of books that people might not buy. If someone wants your book, it's printed; it's a simple as that.

Need2Know

Of course, it's also more expensive doing it that way (which is one reason traditional publishers don't do it) and the shipping costs can be high. It also means that – as author – the hard work of writing a book doesn't end with the last full-stop. You'll be responsible for cover-design, typesetting (simple enough using Lulu's software) as well as sales and marketing.

For more information and a step-by-step guide to self publishing take a look at *Self Publishing – The Essential Guide* by Samantha Pearce (Need2Know).

Exercise 12.3

If you haven't already done so, have a look at Lulu.com now. Sign up for an account – it's free – and have a play with their software. It can be revealing to see how your book might look even if you intend to go down the traditional publishing route when it's finished, and it'll begin to give you some insight into what is – for most authors – post-production of their work.

Money, money, money

Some books sell themselves; if you're well-known for misbehaving in West End night-clubs or parading in front of several million voyeurs on programmes like 'Big Brother' then you'll find the media beating a path to your door once they know you've got a book out. (Whether you've written the book yourself or whether it's any good won't matter!) But for the rest of us, selling our wares is essential – and this goes for everyone, however they're published. Even if Harper Collins makes you an offer you can't refuse, they'll expect you to be heavily involved with the publicity and promotional activities they've got planned. But then, at least they've planned them. If you're doing it alone, you've got to be your own publicist as well, and we'll discuss some of the dark arts of self-promotion at the end of this chapter.

Whatever happens, don't assume that once your book hits the shelves you'll be instantly handing in your resignation from the day job. Authors in the UK earn an average of £16,531 according to a recent survey. But the top 10% of them earn more than 90% of total income made from writing, while the bottom 90% earn less than 10% of it. And – at least in some cases – for 'author' read 'celebrity employing a ghost-writer'. Cynical? Me? Possibly.

You're so vain

I bet you think this book is about you? Don't you? Seriously though, while we're on the subject of publishing, self-publishing, Lulu, money and the like, may I make one thing clear? If someone asks you to pay – 'contribute towards' – the costs of publication don't go anywhere near it.

Ok, so if you want an ISBN and certain distribution packages with Lulu, for example, then you'll have to pay for them. But paying for an ISBN isn't the same as paying for the editing, printing, marketing, distributing and storing of your book and there are plenty of outfits out there who'll send you flattering letters before asking you to stump up at least a grand for a modest print-run of, say, 500 books. Don't go there.

If you're desperate to see yourself in print, go to Lulu or Amazon *Createspace*, where you pay your own costs, and take your own profits. In the world of books and publishing there are seldom areas of complete agreement on anything – except vanity publishing. It's always a bad idea, in spite of the fact that – historically – several well-known authors did it. They had to. They didn't have Lulu.

Sell, sell, sell

If your goal is publication and you've achieved your ambition, it might be tempting to think that's it – job done! But in many ways, the hard work is only just beginning. As mentioned earlier, publishers of all shapes and sizes will expect an author to be as active – maybe even more so – than they themselves are where publicity is concerned. Fortunately, there are several things you can do to help – and don't wait until you've seen your book on the shelves. Start now. Build what publishers like to call your 'author platform'; connect with potential readers; it'll all make selling – when the time comes – so much easier.

Blogging

If you haven't already got a blog, start one. There's no easier way to showcase your talent and talk to your readers. There are currently around 150 million blogs on the Internet and about 150,000 new blogs are created worldwide every day. That's about 1.4 blogs per second! Blogging is big and being part of it can be exciting, satisfying and – sometimes – financially rewarding.

But what is a blog? A blog, or 'weblog' is simply a type of website. It differs from other websites by typically being more dynamic – bloggers update their sites more frequently, sometimes daily or even more; blogs are also interactive – readers often leave comments and create their own on-line discussions – and blogs are often multi-media platforms, featuring photos, videos, podcasts as well as text.

For more information about blogging and a set-by-step guide, take a look at *Blogging – The Essential Guide* by Antonia Chitty and Erica Douglas (Need2Know).

Facebook

With over 800 million active users worldwide, over half of whom log on every day, Facebook has got to be one of the best ways of building an author platform. There are two ways you can proceed: either open a personal account (or use one you've already created) to give readers information about your writing, or create an author page. The latter might be slightly more effective because instead of sending and accepting friend requests users simply 'like' a Facebook page and then receive updates. Here's a link to mine if you'd like to see how it's done: http://www.facebook.com/AuthorTimAtkinson.

Twitter

Of all the so-called social networks available to authors, Twitter is probably the most divisive. People either love it or they hate it; if you sign up for it, you'll need to be pretty active if you want to attract and keep people following your time line. But the great advantage is that – in just 140 characters – you can give quick updates, post links, photos, even video clips and keep people in touch with what you're doing even when you're on the move. It also seems to be the network that attracts most media attention. We've all read about its role in the so-called 'Arab Spring' uprising, but even the recent Jeremy Clarkson outburst against striking public sector workers was probably only picked up by the media because – within seconds – it was trending on Twitter. I'm @dotterel by the way, if you'd like to sign up. Say hello and I'll be happy to show you around.

An age-old problem

Of course, whatever you decide to do about getting published – in fact, whatever you decide about writing in general – don't be in a hurry. I remember hearing Ian Rankin talking about writing on the occasion of his fiftieth birthday. He said that one of the great things about being a writer was the fact that age meant nothing, unlike in many other forms of entertainment. In fact, there's a case for saying that the older you get, the better you write. There's certainly no rush, especially if you're writing in the longer forms like fiction or memoir. Writing is a marathon, not a sprint. But just as you wouldn't attempt a marathon without training, you can't expect to suddenly sit down and complete a novel without at least a little limbering up first.

So, what next?

There are any number of places to go and things to do. Some cost money; some don't; have a look at all of them and decide which is the right step for you.

Study

The Open University runs a variety of Creative Writing courses, from introductory short units like 'Start Writing Fiction' [Start writing fiction (A174)] to full-blown degree-level courses like A215 Creative Writing (http://www.open.ac.uk/Arts/a215/index.html) and A363 Advanced Creative Writing (http://www3.open.ac.uk/study/undergraduate/course/a363.htm).

If all that sounds a bit too daunting, take a look at the BBC's Writersroom which has forums, writing tips and general support in addition to the detailed advice you'll need if you're submitting to the BBC: http://www.bbc.co.uk/writersroom/.

Evening Classes

Creative writing classes and groups exist up and down the country and are often among the most popular at the institutions running them. You can view a directory of them here: http://www.hotcourses.com/uk-courses/Creative-Writing-courses/hc2_browse.pg_loc_tree/16180339/0/p_type_id/1/p_bcat_id/1617/page.htm.

Websites

How To Write A Novel is about, well, how to write a novel but also so much more. Find it here: http://oldenoughnovel.blogspot.com/.

Another site doing what it says on the banner is *Help! I Need a Publisher*. The book of the blog *Write to Be Published* by Nicola Morgan (who knows what she's on about, with books almost into three figures) is out soon. Until then, check the blog here: http://helpineedapublisher.blogspot.com/.

If inspiration ever wanes, a site like this – http://writeidea.wordpress.com/ – might come in handy. Linda Frear doesn't quite manage a different writing prompt each day, but she comes pretty close.

One of the most comprehensive sites, constantly up-dated (I'm talking up to a dozen times daily!) and linking to writing sites all over the world is The Creative Penn: http://www.thecreativepenn.com/. If Joanna Penn doesn't cover it herself, she'll know somebody who does and she'll have linked to them, interviewed them or otherwise distributed their pearls of wisdom somewhere on her well-indexed site.

The final curtain

I can't quite believe the adventure that has been the writing of this book is almost over. The end is near. But we don't face the final curtain. Oh no. Although we're all doing it our way, we're going to keep on doing it, and do it some more. So, whatever you do, keep writing!

Summing Up

▪ Publication is changing and there has probably never been a more exciting time to be an author.

▪ Although traditional routes to publications still exist, eBooks and online publication, together with self-publishing options, mean the chances of seeing your work in print have never been better.

▪ Remember – once the book is printed, the hard work isn't over. Think about the ways of increasing your online presence: start a blog, create a Facebook page, join Twitter.

Help List

On the following pages you'll find a list of some helpful resources ranging from websites, author pages, 'how to write' books as well as examples of fine writing from many of the genres discussed in this book.

Useful Websites

Authonomy
www.authonomy.com/

BBC Writer's Room
www.bbc.co.uk/writersroom/

CompletelyNovel
www.completelynovel.com/

Dotterel Press
www.dotterelpress.com/

Help! I Need a Publisher
www.helpineedapublisher.blogspot.com/

How To Write A Novel
www.oldenoughnovel.blogspot.com/

Me and my Big Mouth
www.meandmybigmouth.typepad.com/scottpack/

The Creative Penn
www.thecreativepenn.com/

The Literary Consultancy

www.literaryconsultancy.co.uk/

The Write Idea

writeidea.wordpress.com/

WriteThisMoment

www.writethismoment.com/

Writing Forward

www.writingforward.com/

Useful magazines

Writers' Forum

www.writers-forum.com
Inspiring how-to articles on writing, plus competitions.

Writing Magazine (now combined with Writers' News)

Tel: 0113 200 2929
www.writersnews.co.uk
Competitions, articles on every aspect of writing short stories, as well as marketing – plus news of likely magazine markets for writers.

Conferences

Southern Writers' Conference

Independent at Earnly, annual in June.
Earnley, Chichester, West Sussex PO20 7JN
Secretary: Lucia White Tel: 01396 876202

Swanwick, Writers' Summer School (annual in August)

The Hayes Conference Centre, Swanwick, Derbyshire.
Secretary: Fiona McFadzean, 40 Pemberton Valley, AYR, KA7 4UB
Tel: 01292 442786

The Earnley Concourse

Various writing courses, year-round, check website.
Earnley, Chichester, West Sussex, PO20 7JN
Email: info@earnley.co.uk Tel:01243 670392

Writers' Holiday

Various courses and venues, UK and Spain, check website.
www.malagaworkshops.co.uk
Course Organiser: Lois Maddox Tel: 01454 773579

Additional author resources

The Society of Authors

www.societyofauthors.org
An independent trade union representing writers' interests and offering
specialist advice and support for members

The Writers' Guild

www.writersguild.org.uk
A TUC-affiliated trade union for writers.

The Arvon Foundation

www.arvonfoundation.org
Charity providing writing course and retreats for writers in a variety of locations

Copyright Licensing Agency (CLA)

www.cla.co.uk
This body arranges and authorises use of copyright material where authors
require it.

Crime Writer's Association

www.thecwa.co.uk
Best known for the famous 'Dagger' awards, the CWA is the umbrella organisation for writers of crime fiction

National Association of Writers in Education (NAWE)

www.nawe.co.uk
As well as providing a database of UK creative writing courses, the NAWE supports the development of creative writing across the educational spectrum

Romantic Novelists Association

www.rna-uk.org
Working to support those writing and seeking to write romantic fiction, the NRA operates a scheme for the appraisal of new manuscripts

Bibliography

Becoming a Writer
Dorothea Brande (Tarcher 1981)
ISBN: 978-0874771640

The Art of Fiction
David Lodge (Vintage 2011)
ISBN: 978-0099554240

Creating Fictional Characters
Jean Saunders (Need2Know, 2011)
ISBN: 978-1-86144-120-1

Publishing Poetry
Kenneth Steven (Need2Know, 2010)
ISBN: 978-1-86144-113-3

How Novels Work
John Mullan (OUP 2008)
ISBN: 978-0199281787

Plot and Structure: Techniques and Exercises
James Scott Bell (Writer's Digest, 2005)
ISBN: 978-1582972947

What If? Writing Exercises for Fiction Writers
Anne Bernays (Harper Collins 2005)
ISBN: 978-0062720061

Writing Romantic Fiction
Jean Saunders (Need2Know, 2011)
ISBN: 978-1-86144-121-8

Writing Non-Fiction Books
Gordon Wells (Need2Know, 2010)
ISBN: 978-1-86144-114-0

Writing Poetry
W.N.Herbert (Routledge 2009)
ISBN: 978-0415461542

The Five-Minute Writer
Margaret Geraghty (How To Books Ltd 2009)
ISBN: 978-1845283391

Writing Therapy
Tim Atkinson (Dotterel Press 2009)
ISBN: 978-0-9562869-0-1

Writers' and Artists' Yearbook
(A & C Black 2011)
ISBN: 978-1408135808

Writer's Handbook
ed. Barry Turner (Palgrave 2010)
ISBN: 978-0230207295

Writers Market 2012
ed. Robert Lee Brewer (Writer's Digest Books 2011)
ISBN: 978-1599632261

Self-editing for Fiction Writers: How to Edit Yourself into Print
Browne, Renni, and Dave King. (Harper Resource, 2004)
ISBN: 978-0060545697

How Not to Write a Novel: 200 Mistakes to Avoid at All Costs If You Ever Want to Get Published
Mittelmark and Newman (Penguin, 2009)
ISBN: 978-0141038544

On Writing: A Memoir of the Craft
Steven King (New English Library 2001)
ISBN: 978-0340820469

Strong Words: Modern Poets on Modern Poetry
W.N.Herbert and Matthew Hollis (Bloodaxe, 2000)
ISBN: 978-1852245153

The following books are examples of work by the authors quoted above and represent good examples of writing from some of the styles and genres mentioned:

The Hating Game
Talli Roland (Prospera 2011)
ISBN: 978-1907504037

Build a Man (Kindle ed.)
Talli Roland (Notting Hill Press 2011)
ASIN: B00642BCX2

My So-Called Afterlife
Tamsyn Murray (Piccadilly Press 2010)
ISBN: 978-1848120570

Sue Guiney, A Clash of Innocents
(Ward Wood 2010)
ISBN: 978-0956660206

Bad Shaman Blues
W.N.Herbert (Bloodaxe 2006)
ISBN: 978-1852247287

If I Never
Gary William Murning (Legend Press 2009)
ISBN: 978-1906558147

Children of the Resolution
Gary William Murning (Lulu 2010)
ISBN: 978-1446650202

Roman Britain: A New History
Guy de la Bédoyère (Thames and Hudson 2010)
ISBN: 978-0500287484

Writing Therapy (Kindle ed)
Tim Atkinson (Dotterel Press 2011)
ASIN: B004MDLPYQ

Need - 2 - Know

Available Titles Include ...

Publishing Poetry The Essential Guide
ISBN 978-1-86144-113-3 £9.99

Pilates The Essential Guide
ISBN 978-1-86144-097-6 £9.99

Writing Poetry The Essential Guide
ISBN 978-1-86144-112-6 £9.99

Surfing The Essential Guide
ISBN 978-1-86144-106-5 £9.99

Writing Non-Fiction Books The Essential Guide
ISBN 978-1-86144-114-0 £9.99

Gardening A Beginner's Guide
ISBN 978-1-86144-100-3 £9.99

Book Proposals The Essential Guide
ISBN 978-1-86144-118-8 £9.99

Going Green The Essential Guide
ISBN 978-1-86144-089-1 £9.99

Writing Dialogue The Essential Guide
ISBN 978-1-86144-119-5 £9.99

Food for Health The Essential Guide
ISBN 978-1-86144-095-2 £9.99

Creating Fictional Characters The Essential Guide
ISBN 978-1-86144-120-1 £9.99

Vegan Cookbook The Essential Guide
ISBN 978-1-86144-123-2 £9.99

Writing Romantic Fiction The Essential Guide
ISBN 978-1-86144-121-8 £9.99

Walking A Beginner's Guide
ISBN 978-1-86144-101-0 £9.99

View the full range at **www.need2knowbooks.co.uk**. To order our titles call **01733 898103**,
email **sales@n2kbooks.com** or visit the website. Selected ebooks available online.

Need - 2 - Know, Remus House, Coltsfoot Drive, Peterborough, PE2 9BF